BIBLE
DEVOTIONS
FOR
BEDTIME

Daniel Partner

HUMBLECREEK
INSPIRATION FOR LIFE

Interior illustrations by Ken Save and Kathy Arbuckle.

Published by Barbour Publishing, Inc., P.O. Box 719, Uhrichsville, Ohio 44683
www.barbourbooks.com

Our mission is to publish and distribute inspirational products offering exceptional value and biblical encouragement to the masses.

ecpa Member of the
Evangelical Christian
Publishers Association

Printed in the United States of America.
5 4 3 2 1

INTRODUCTION FOR PARENTS

One day some parents brought their children to Jesus. They wanted him to touch them and bless them. But the disciples told these people, "Don't bother him." When Jesus saw this, he was very unhappy. He said to his disciples, "Let the children come to me. Don't stop them! For the Kingdom of God belongs to such as these" (Mark 10:13–14 NLT). This shows that a few people had the good sense to take their children to Jesus while they could! Today it takes the same good sense to bring one's children to the Bible.

The book you have in your hands introduces your child to the Bible. And with your prayer, the Bible can help lead your child to Jesus. Here are over three hundred brief thoughts about the Old and New Testaments. They tell of the Creation of the world; Adam, Eve, and their fall from God; and the many characters and events of the book of Genesis. Here are introductions to the children of Israel, Pharaoh, and Moses. Stories of the plagues of Egypt, the Exodus, and the birth of Christ are here, too. Ruth, Hannah, Samuel, David, Elijah, Mary, Joseph, and many other personalities are here. Chief among these is Jesus Christ.

Each person and story in this book contains a seed of truth that can grow in a child's heart. Read these together with your children and plant these precious seeds in their hearts.

This book has been written for an elementary level reader. But the Bible isn't *The Cat in the Hat*. It is a complex book with high, heavenly concepts. So, although some children will be able to read the stories here, all will need an adult's guidance. I've used simple language; still, there are words and sentences that will need your explanation. Events like humanity's fall, Noah's flood, and Christ's death and resurrection should be explained further than do the words of this book.

Little boys and girls desperately need their parents by their side. Young hearts are strengthened and reassured by their parents' warm touch and the resonance of their voice. So use this book as an excuse to pause and sit with your child, and enjoy the quiet moments while you consider its important ideas. Have a Bible at hand and look up some verses. Let your child see you handle God's Word and let him or her do the same.

Make your time with your children a gift—like God's salvation—and they'll long to remember and treasure the truth of the gospel contained in the simple words of this book.

Daniel Partner
Coos Bay, Oregon
September 1, 2004

THE STARTING POINT

In the beginning God created the heavens and the earth.
GENESIS 1:1 NLT

When you read a book, it is important to know what that book is about. This is not hard to do. Sometimes the name of the book tells you. The book called *The Cat in the Hat* is about a cat wearing a hat. There is a book called *The Adventures of Peter Rabbit*. It is a book about exciting things that happen to a rabbit named Peter. And the name *The Cat in the Hat Comes Back* tells you just what that book is about.

What do you think the Bible is about? The word *bible* means "book." That name doesn't give a hint about what's inside the book. But read the first four words of the Bible: "In the beginning God. . ." Do these words tell you what the Bible is about? Yes! The Bible is about God.

True, the Bible tells about many things and many people. But all in all, the Bible is meant to show you who God is and what God has done for you.

Dear God, thank you for the Bible, which tells me all about you.

GOD MADE LIGHT

And God said, "Let there be light," and there was light.

What is the first thing you see when you wake up in the morning? Maybe you see your blankets or the ceiling of your room. Maybe you see a stuffed animal or toys on your bed.

But before you answer my question, read about the first thing that God made: "And God said, 'Let there be light,' and there was light." The very first day of God's Creation began with light. This is just like the beginning of every day in your life. When you open your eyes there is light. Maybe it comes from the sun shining in your window. It could come from a light bulb in a lamp. Or a little bit of light may come through your open bedroom door. This light helps you to see what is around you—your room, your toys, and the clothes you will wear that day.

Every day of your life is a gift from God. Each of your days begins just like the first day of God's Creation. It begins with light.

Dear God, thank you for giving us light for each new day.

AFRAID OF THE DARK?

And he separated the light from the darkness.
God called the light "day," and the darkness he called "night."
GENESIS 1:4–5 NIV

Some children are afraid of the dark. That's why there are night lights. They let us put some light into the darkness. Then you can see just a little bit if you wake up at night. Do you know the first thing the Bible says about darkness? It says, "And he separated the light from the darkness. God called the light 'day,' and the darkness he called 'night.' "

Maybe you're wondering, "Why is there darkness if kids are afraid of it?" God probably has many reasons for this. Can you think of some of these reasons? Sleep is one good reason. Can you fall asleep in the daylight as well as in the dark? How would you decide when to sleep if there were no night? Maybe people would be sleeping at all different times! Also, sunrise is when a day begins, and after sunset it ends. So light starts a day and darkness ends each day.

There is another reason for darkness and all the other things God made: They are part of God's Creation, so they are a part of God's plan.

Dear God, help me when I am afraid of the dark. Help me to remember that you made the dark and it is part of your plan.

CREATION'S PLAN

And God said, "Let the water under the sky be gathered to one place,
and let dry ground appear." And it was so.

GENESIS 1:9 NIV

God made the heavens and the earth for a reason. They are part of his plan. The book of Genesis, the first book of the Bible, says that God took seven days to make the earth. This is called Creation.

On the second day of Creation, God made the sky. But the whole earth was still covered with water! Then something very important happened on the third day. "And God said, 'Let the water under the sky be gathered to one place, and let the dry land appear.' And it was so." This made it possible for other wonderful things to happen. All kinds of plants and trees began to grow! Here's what the Bible says about this: "The land produced vegetation: plants bearing seed according to their kinds and trees bearing fruit with seed in it according to their kinds. And God saw that it was good."

Have you seen that there is neatness in what God has done? God's work is orderly. First God made light, then the sky and water. Next came the dry land so that plants could grow. God's work was peaceful and simple. As the Bible says, "God is not a God of disorder but of peace."

Dear God, thank you for being a God of peace and order.

SUN, MOON, AND STARS

And God said, "Let bright lights appear in the sky."
GENESIS 1:14 NLT

It is good that the sky is not empty. How boring that would be! All day long, we would see only blue sky. And at night, we would see nothing but black. God wanted more than this. So the Bible says, "God made two great lights, the sun and the moon, to shine down upon the earth. The greater one, the sun, presides during the day; the lesser one, the moon, presides through the night. He also made the stars."

The greater light rules the day. What is that light? It is the sun. The lesser light rules the night. What do you think this is? That's easy! It is the moon. And God made the stars, too.

On the first day there was light. But God wanted more than just that light. So He made the sun and moon and stars on the fourth day. You may be able to think of some reasons for these lights in the sky. They're very pretty, aren't they? The sunshine is so warm, and it makes things grow.

The Bible gives reasons for the sun, moon, and stars. It says that the sun divides the day from the night. The changing shape of the moon and patterns of the stars are sometimes helpful, kind of like road signs. And all three mark the changing seasons, days, and years. God said this was good. Don't you think so, too?

Dear God, thank you for the sun, the moon, and the stars.

ANiMALS, ANiMALS EVERYWHERE

So God created great sea creatures and every sort of fish and every kind of bird.
God made all sorts of wild animals, livestock, and small animals.
GENESIS 1:21, 25 NLT

Do you like animals? If you answered "yes," that's great! Because on the fifth day, God made the waters swarm with fish and other life. And the skies were filled with birds of every kind. God created big sea creatures, too. Think about all the different kinds of birds and fish there are. God made each one! God saw that this was good and He blessed them all.

Wait, there's more!

The next day, God decided that there should be all kinds of other animals. So God made livestock like cattle, sheep, and goats. He made small animals and other wildlife. Plus, he made all the things that creep on the ground, like bugs and snakes and lizards.

Just about everything was made by this time, right? There was earth and sky and sea. The sun, moon, and stars were shining bright. Plants and trees and grass grew fresh and green. And there were animals everywhere, on land and in the sea and sky.

Could anything be missing? Think about it. . . . Yes, something is missing. *You* aren't there! There are no people yet. That's coming up next!

Dear God, I love the animals that you made—thank you for all of them!

MADE FOR ME

Then God said, "Let us make people in our image,
to be like ourselves. They will be masters over all life."
GENESIS 1:26 NLT

What do you see when you look out your window? I see the blue sky peeking through a tree's branches and leaves. The tree grows on a low slope covered with different kinds of bushes, grasses, and plants. Everything is shades of green. Some purple flowers bloom on a bush. A golden hummingbird visits little orange flowers scattered here and there. Yellow bees buzz by. Sometimes a big black dragonfly flies in and stops in midair. The sunshine makes shadows. The breeze from the ocean makes them jiggle and shake. A silvery spider's web shimmers in the window frame.

God made all this and more—more than anyone can even imagine! Have you ever thought about why the heavens and the earth are here? Why is the earth covered with living things? Here's why: God worked for the first five days of Creation to get ready for the sixth day. That is the day God made people.

Remember the taste of your favorite food and the smell you like the best. Imagine the softest thing you know—a kitten's fur, a feather, the petal of a flower. God made these and all things just for you!

Dear God, thank you for everything I can see, hear, smell, and touch.

VERY GOOD

God saw all that he had made, and it was very good. And there was evening,
and there was morning—the sixth day.
GENESIS 1:31 NIV

Genesis chapter one tells about all the things God created. Each day of Creation was different. God started with light and darkness and then made everything else. He made the sky, the land, the sea. He made plants and animals. Finally, God made the best part of Creation—human beings like you and me.

Something different happened on each day of Creation. But this chapter of the Bible also repeats something over and over again. It says, "God saw that it was good." Twice on the third day, God saw that it was good. And on the fourth and fifth days, God saw that it was good. After the animals were made on the sixth day, God saw that it was good. Five times the Bible says, "God saw that it was good." What does this tell you? It means that God's Creation is good!

Then people were added to Creation and the Bible says something a little different: "God saw all that he had made, and it was very good." When we were made the Creation was finished. Then the world was not only good, it was *very* good!

Dear God, thank you for making me and all of your Creation very good!

TiME TO REST

On the seventh day, having finished his task,
God rested from all his work.
GENESIS 2:2 NLT

The Bible tells about God's power. And God is strong, too. But God is much more than powerful and strong. God is also holy, eternal, faithful, wise, true, and good. God is light. God is love. God is so much that there are not enough words to tell it all!

The Bible is the book that tells us all we need to know about God. The first thing it says is that God is the Creator, and it tells the story of Creation. And there are not just six days in the Creation story. It took God seven days to finish making everything. The first six days were for working. Then on the seventh day, God rested from all his work. First, God worked to create everything. What is the second thing the Bible tells about God? It says that God rested. But God is so strong and powerful. Why would he need to rest? Maybe to help us remember that we should take time to rest, too!

Dear God, thank you for being who you are—powerful, holy, and full of love.

PAY ATTENTION!

This is the account of the heavens and the earth when they were created.

GENESIS 2:4 NIV

Genesis tells the story of Creation twice. The first time was in chapter one, and the story is told again in chapter two. Every book and chapter of the Bible is important. Even each word is important. Though chapter two of Genesis tells about Creation again, it can't be skipped.

The second Creation story tells about the first man and woman, Adam and Eve. It tells how God made them and the place where they lived. They lived in a garden in a place called Eden. A river flowed through Eden and trees grew there. Two of these trees were very important—the tree of life and the tree of the knowledge of good and evil. The second Creation story also tells how Adam named all the animals and about Adam's and Eve's wedding!

Sometimes in school your teacher says, "Pay attention!" These two words give good advice. When reading the Bible you have to pay attention, especially when it says things twice.

Dear God, thank you for the Bible and for helping us pay attention to your Word.

FIRST THINGS FIRST

No plant of the field had yet sprung up, for the Lord God had not sent rain on the earth and there was no man to work the ground.

GENESIS 2:5 NIV

The Bible is a book of wisdom. It helps us learn how to live our lives. The words of this verse give us wisdom for our lives.

At first, it didn't rain at all in the Garden of Eden. Imagine a time when there was no rain or snow, sleet, or hail. Nothing wet came from the sky. It's a good thing that there was a stream bringing water to the Garden of Eden!

Do you know why God didn't send the rain? There was no one to plow the earth like a farmer does. And without rain, nothing will grow. But the rain wouldn't come unless someone worked on the land. First comes work, then comes rain, finally things grow. That's the wisdom here.

You can use this wisdom in your life. Do you want to get good grades in school? Sure you do. But what if you don't do your school work? You get poor grades. First you must do your work, then you can get good grades.

Dear God, help me to work hard for you.

FORMED, NOT MADE

And the LORD God formed a man's body from the dust of the ground and breathed into it the breath of life. And the man became a living person.

GENESIS 2:7 NLT

This verse gives us a lot to think about. It tells about how people came to be here. First, it says that God formed us. All the other creatures were created and made. But we human beings were *formed*.

Have you ever formed something out of clay? You soften the clay

 with the warmth of your hands. You roll it or cut it. You shape it and reshape it. You work with the clay until it becomes what you want it to be.

People were to be different from the rest of Creation. This is why the Bible uses a new word to describe how we came to be. It says, "God formed man." It didn't happen fast. God worked step-by-step and was very careful when he made us. This shows how important we are in

God's plan. God worked to make us right and beautiful. Another part of the Bible says, "Lord, you are our Father. We are the clay, and you are the potter. We are all formed by your hand."

Dear God, thank you for taking the time to make me special.

A SPECIAL PLACE

Then the LORD God planted a garden in Eden, in the east,
and there he placed the man he had created.
GENESIS 2:8 NLT

The first people God created were named Adam and Eve. They lived in a garden in Eden. This was a huge place. All the animals were there; trees and plants were growing; and rivers were flowing. Gold and precious stones were there. It must have been more beautiful than anything we've ever seen!

There God brought the animals and birds to the first man. Adam gave them all names. Imagine that! Adam was so smart that he could give a different name to every animal. He knew each and every one. Adam cared for the garden by working as a farmer. And it was there in the garden that God made the woman, Eve. The two were married in the Garden of Eden.

If you like animals, you would have liked that garden. If you like flowers and trees, Eden was the place for you. What would you do there? You could swim in the rivers. You could collect precious stones. You could climb trees. You could plant and grow things. You could live with the animals.

All these things are wonderful. But they are not what really made Eden so wonderful. Here is why Eden was so good: God walked there in the cool evenings. He spoke to Adam and Eve, and they talked to him. God was there, so it was paradise!

Dear God, thank you for our planet, but most of all for your presence.

RULES

Eden was a wonderful paradise because God was there. Everything in that big garden was free to Adam and Eve. And all the trees were "pleasing to the eye and good for food." Two special trees had

names. One was called the tree of life. The other was the tree of the knowledge of good and evil.

So Adam and Eve lived there together with God. They had the rivers and plants, trees and precious stones, and all the animals. But even in that perfect place, there was one rule: Don't eat from the tree of the knowledge of good and evil. It is good to remember that there are always rules and laws to follow. They keep us safe.

If you or I were in Eden we would have eaten fruit from every tree. But if we ate from the tree of the knowledge of good and evil, we would have died. That was a dangerous tree. So God made a good rule: "You must not eat from the tree of the knowledge of good and evil." This rule kept Adam and Eve safe, just like rules today are meant to keep us safe.

Dear God, thank you for taking care of me and making rules to keep me safe.

ALONE OR TOGETHER?

And the LORD God said, "It is not good for the man to be alone.
I will make a companion who will help him."
GENESIS 2:18 NLT

The very first man was all alone in that great big garden. God knew this, and he cared that Adam was alone. So God made all the animals and brought them to Adam. Was this how God wanted to fill Adam's loneliness? Were the animals to be Adam's companions on this earth?

Adam must have looked at each animal very carefully. After all, he gave each one a name. Giraffe, pig, alligator, dog, cat, elephant. How many kinds of animals are there? Tens of thousands, maybe millions. Adam knew them all. But after he had given them each a name, he was still alone. Adam still did not have a wife, someone to be his friend and helper in life.

There were so many wonderful animals. Adam must have enjoyed them. But no animal was right to be Adam's lifelong mate. What would you do to keep Adam from being alone? God did one final thing in order to complete the Creation. God made a woman.

Dear God, thank you for making a helper for Adam.

VERY SMART

So the LORD God formed from the soil every kind of animal and bird.
He brought them to Adam to see what he would call them,
and Adam chose a name for each one.

GENESIS 2:19 NLT

Do you know someone who you think is smart? This could be your mother or father, or a family member. Certainly, your schoolteacher knows a lot more than you do. But Adam was *very* smart. God brought all the animals to him. Then Adam chose a name for each one. Think of the names of as many animals as you can. How many animal names do you know? How many animal names does your father or mother know? How about your teacher?

Adam didn't just know every animal name, he is the one who gave all the animals their names! This means that he named every farm animal, every bird, and every wild animal. Adam probably named all the bugs and fish, too. This shows that God made people to be very, very smart!

Dear God, thank you for making me so smart!

SOMETHING NEW

So the LORD God caused Adam to fall into a deep sleep.
He took one of Adam's ribs. . . . Then the LORD God made a woman
from the rib and brought her to Adam.
GENESIS 2:21–22 NLT

Think of all that God did to make the heavens and the earth. When God spoke the word, there was light and day and night, the sky and the dry land and the sea. When God spoke, the sun, moon, and stars appeared in the sky. Over and over again Genesis tells us, "And God said." That's how the Creation appeared—grass, herbs, and trees; fish and birds and even huge whales. All this happened because God spoke!

Then God changed the way of Creation. "And the Lord God formed a man's body from the dust of the ground and breathed into it the breath of life. And the man became a living person." God didn't just speak to make Adam. God worked to form him from dust. Then, so that Adam would have life, God breathed into him.

But Adam could not be alone. He needed a mate, someone who matched him in every way. This is why God made woman in a new and different way. God didn't speak or use dust, like before. Unlike everything else, woman was made from a part of Adam. And Adam said, "She is part of my own flesh and bone! She will be called 'woman,' because she was taken out of a man."

Dear God, thank you for giving the breath of life to Adam—and to me!

A SAD STORY

Now the serpent was the shrewdest of all the creatures the LORD God had made. "Really?" he asked the woman. "Did God really say you must not eat any of the fruit in the garden?"
GENESIS 3:1 NLT

The Bible is full of stories. Many of these are about good people who do good things. Bible stories tell of brave men and women and of people with courage and love. The Bible also tells stories of what God has done and will do for us.

But the Bible tells some sad stories, too. The saddest story tells how Adam and Eve failed God. It shows them leaving the wonderful Garden of Eden. We see them here for the first time living without God. This is the worst thing that could happen to them and to us.

There were many different kinds of trees in the garden. God said that the man and woman could eat the fruit of all those trees except for one—the tree of the knowledge of good and evil. This seems simple, doesn't it? But a powerful enemy of God entered Eden looking like a snake. This snake asked Eve which trees she could eat fruit from. It was a simple question, and Eve knew the right answer. But the snake tempted Eve to eat the forbidden fruit anyway, and this was the beginning of the fall of humanity into sin. Soon, our simple, beautiful life with God would end.

Dear God, help me to do what makes you happy—help me to do what is right.

RiGHT AND WRONG

"But God did say, 'You must not eat fruit from the tree that is in the middle
of the garden, and you must not touch it, or you will die.'"
"You will not surely die," the serpent said to the woman.
GENESIS 3:3–4 NIV

Hurray for Eve! She knew what God had said about the tree of the knowledge of good and evil. If they ate of it they would die. But what did that snake do? The snake lied to her, "You won't die."

What was Eve to do? Adam wasn't nearby. Maybe he was away tending another part of the garden. So she could not ask Adam about the snake's lie.

Eve knew that God had said, "If you eat from that tree, you will die." Suddenly, because of the snake's lie, she was mixed up about this. All at once, she didn't know what to think. Would she die or not?

If Eve were here now, she would tell us what to learn from what happened to her. First, she would tell us always to remember God's Word and never let it go, even when others tell you something different. And second, if you are not sure if something is right or wrong, talk to other people about it. Ask your parents or another grown-up. Most of all, ask God to help you know what he wants you to do.

Dear God, help me to know what is right and wrong.

DYING

So she ate some of the fruit. She also gave some to her husband,
who was with her. Then he ate it, too.

GENESIS 3:6 NLT

A terrible thing happened when Adam and Eve ate the fruit of the only tree that God told them not to eat from. The people of the Garden of Eden died! God said this would happen if they ate of that tree. And it did happen.

It may not seem to you that they died. After all, they didn't drop dead after eating the fruit. Since this is true, it teaches that there are two kinds of death. One comes when our body dies. When our body is dead, we cannot live in this world anymore. But this is not what happened to Adam and Eve. After they ate the fruit, they knew their bodies were naked, and so they made clothes out of leaves. So we know they were still alive in their bodies.

But there is another kind of death.

Think of pretty flowers in a vase. They have all their color, and they may even smell good. They seem to be alive, but they are not. These flowers have been cut off from their roots in the soil. They can't get their food from the earth anymore. In time, they will wilt away. In fact, they are already dead.

In the same way, Adam and Eve were cut off from God. That's what God meant when he said they would die if they ate the forbidden fruit.

Dear God, teach me to be alive in you—to trust what you say.

HiDiNG FROM GOD

Then the man and his wife heard the sound of the LORD God. . .
and they hid from the LORD God among the trees of the garden.
GENESIS 3:8 NIV

This is a very sad verse. Adam was hiding from God. He had been formed by God's hands out of the dust and made in God's image. He was like a beautiful clay bowl, hand-painted by God. Yet he was living. Life had come into him with God's breath. Adam had walked with God, spoken to God, listened to God's voice—but now he was hiding from God.

The woman, Eve, was there, too—the one who made God's Creation complete. She was nearby her husband, hiding from God. Why? Because Adam and Eve were afraid. They knew they had done the one thing God said they should not do. They ate the fruit of the tree of the knowledge of good and evil. They wondered what would happen next. God had said they would die. Was he going to kill them? No wonder they were afraid!

These are such sad words, "they hid from the LORD God." This is called the Fall of man. Suddenly Adam and Eve had to use the garden's trees for protection instead of food. Paradise was past.

Dear God, help me to remember that if I obey you, I don't need to be afraid of you.

WHEN GOD SPEAKS

"Have you eaten the fruit I commanded you not to eat?"

GENESIS 3:11 NLT

Do you remember that God said Adam and Eve would die if they ate from the wrong tree? But God didn't kill Adam. Instead, God asked, "Did you eat from that tree?" This tells something about God. God wants to talk with you and hear from you, even when you've done something wrong. In other words, God won't give up on you.

Adam did the one forbidden thing. So he was suddenly afraid of God, and he hid from God. But God reached out to Adam and spoke to him. Much later, God would do the same thing for the whole world.

The Bible says, "For God so loved the world that he gave his one and only Son, that whoever believes in him shall not perish but have eternal life. For God did not send his Son into the world to condemn the world, but to save the world through him." By the time these words were written, the whole world had turned away from God. But even then the world wasn't doomed. Why? Because God sent Jesus into the world to bring it back to God. God reached out to us all through Jesus so that we would not be lost.

Dear God, thank you for sending Jesus to save us!

RESPONSIBILITY

Then the LORD God said to the woman,
"What is this you have done?"
GENESIS 3:13 NIV

First God talked to Adam, "Have you eaten from the tree that I commanded you not to eat from?"

Right away, Adam blamed Eve. "The woman you put here with me—she gave me some fruit from the tree, and I ate it."

Then God spoke to Eve, "What is this you have done?" So Eve blamed the snake.

There are a few things to learn from this story. The first lesson is that God will speak to anyone who will listen. God spoke to Adam and also to Eve. Remember, no one stands between you and God.

Here's another lesson: Adam had to answer for what had happened, but he couldn't speak for Eve. The woman had to answer for herself. Both were responsible for what they had done.

And another lesson here is that people blame others when bad things happen. Adam said, "The woman gave me the fruit of that tree." Then Eve said, "The snake tricked me into eating from that tree." But Adam wasn't forced to take the fruit from Eve. He knew he shouldn't eat it. And so did Eve. She didn't have to believe the snake. Blaming others didn't save Adam and Eve.

Remember that you are responsible to God.

Dear God, thank you for loving me and keeping me responsible for my actions.

NEW CLOTHES

Adam named his wife Eve, because she would become the mother of all the living.
The LORD God made garments of skin for Adam and his wife and clothed them.
GENESIS 3:20–21 NIV

Adam and Eve disobeyed God. This is called sin. They ate from the wrong tree so they lost almost everything they had. But they did not lose their lives. This is why the woman was named Eve, "the mother of all living."

But sadly, something did die that day because of Adam and Eve's sin.

God made clothes of animal skins for Adam and Eve. These clothes covered their nakedness. Where did those skins come from? Animals had to die. Maybe these were lambs, whose soft skins make good clothes. No one knows.

Adam must have been so unhappy seeing the death of his beloved animals. Nothing had ever died before this happened. He knew the animals had died because of his sin. The skins of dead animals covered his sinful nakedness.

Those animals died long ago because of sin. But the problem of sin was not solved until about two thousand years ago. Then Jesus Christ also died because of sin. Now, faith in Jesus does more than cover your sin. When you believe that Jesus died for your sin and came back to life, your sin is washed away forever!

Dear God, thank you for washing my sins away through Jesus' blood.

SEPARATION

So the LORD God banished him from the Garden of Eden
to work the ground from which he had been taken.
GENESIS 3:23 NIV

When Adam and Eve sinned, they could not live with God in the garden anymore. They had to leave God—they fell away from God when they sinned.

Why did this have to happen? Remember that the serpent tempted Eve. She ate the fruit of the tree of the knowledge of good and evil. Then she gave some to Adam and he ate it, too. God had told them not to do this. But they disobeyed. Their disobedience was their sin.

What is sin? It is whatever keeps you away from God or from other people.

For example, if you are not nice to people, their feelings are hurt. Then they don't want to be around you. What you did to hurt them keeps them away. This is what happened between Adam and God. And so, our unhappy history began. Adam and Eve were first, but all humanity followed in the Fall from God.

In the Garden of Eden, God gave Adam and Eve everything they needed. All the trees there were beautiful and had good fruit to eat. But after the Fall, Adam and Eve had to leave the garden. Their sin separated them from God and they had to work for everything from then on.

Dear God, forgive me for my sin that separates me from you.

THE TREE OF LIFE

After banishing them from the garden,
the LORD God stationed mighty angelic beings to the east of Eden.
And a flaming sword flashed back and forth, guarding the way to the tree of life.

GENESIS 3:24 NLT

There was another important tree in the Garden of Eden. To understand the Bible, you must know about this tree. It is the tree of life.

Adam and Eve could have chosen to eat from the tree of life.

Instead, they ate from the tree of the knowledge of good and evil. So they died by losing their link with God. This sin also brought death to their bodies. If they had eaten from the tree of life, everything would be different today. There would be no death. We would all be living with God. Everyone would have eternal life.

The way to the tree of life was cut off because Adam sinned. Then there was no way for people to have eternal life. It is a sad story, but there is good news! God did not forget us when Adam sinned. Later, he sent Jesus Christ into the world to show us the way to eternal life. So don't be sad. Believe in Jesus and the way to the tree of life will open to you!

Dear God, thank you for sending your son, Jesus, for me!

SEEDS OF SIN

Eve. . .conceived and gave birth to Cain. . . .
Later she gave birth to his brother Abel.
And while they were in the field,
Cain attacked his brother Abel and killed him.
GENESIS 4:1–2, 8 NIV

After they ate fruit from the wrong tree, God cursed Adam and Eve. He told Adam to go to work. So Adam plowed and planted in the very soil from which he was made. And Eve had two sons named Cain and Abel. God had told her, "You will have children with intense pain and suffering." Though she suffered to give birth, Eve said she was blessed: "With the help of the Lord I have brought forth a man." Even today, children are God's blessing. But with Eve's children, the Fall of man went on.

Do you ever wonder why eating some fruit was so bad? But it was very bad because Adam and Eve disobeyed God, and sin came into the world. Sin was sown into the human heart like a seed, and it grew quickly. By the second generation, it had blossomed and brought forth fruit. That fruit was murder—Cain's murder of Abel.

Some people don't like the Bible because it tells stories like this one. The child of the first man and woman was a murderer. This is true, but many people would rather not know about it. The Bible tells the truth and sometimes the truth hurts. The truth can heal, too. At the right time, the truth of the Bible will heal the whole earth.

Dear God, help me not to disobey you.

CALL ON THE LORD

She gave birth to a son and named him Seth. . . .
Seth also had a son, and he named him Enosh.
At that time men began to call on the name of the LORD.
GENESIS 4:25–26 NIV

Everything that grew in the Garden of Eden was food for Adam and Eve. But outside the garden, they had to find their own food. So Cain became a farmer. In the garden they were naked, and it was okay. But without God, they needed clothing. So Abel raised sheep. This shows our growth away from God.

Man had once found shelter in God. But Genesis chapter four tells of Jabal who made tents. He also raised livestock to aid in farming the land. Also, people no longer found their joy in God. So Jubal made music for enjoyment. Tubal-Cain was the first blacksmith; he made tools of all kinds. He probably made weapons, too. Soon, people began to fight and to kill each other.

Someone, maybe it was Seth, saw that things were going from bad to worse. He realized that people had to get back to God. So then "men began to call on the name of the Lord." And today "everyone who calls on the name of the Lord will be saved."

Dear God, help me to call on you.

ONE GOOD MAN

And he saw that all their thoughts were consistently and totally evil.
So the LORD was sorry he had ever made them. It broke his heart.

GENESIS 6:5—6 NLT

The journey from Genesis chapter three to chapter six is not happy. But in chapter six, things get better. This chapter tells of Noah and the ark—a good story about how God solved the problem of man's wickedness. God saw how bad the people on the earth were, and he was sorry that he had made them. So he decided to destroy every living creature on the earth. "I'll wipe out people, animals, birds, and reptiles," said God.

The bright spot in this story is Noah. He was the only person who lived right and obeyed God. Everyone else, the Bible says, was terribly cruel and violent.

So God told Noah, "Get some wood and build a boat."

You may know how the rest of the story goes. The boat that Noah built was Noah's ark. Noah, his family, and animals of every kind went into the ark. Then it began to rain. It didn't stop raining for forty days! The flood destroyed everything except for what was in the ark. In the end, Noah and his family began a new world.

God judged the human race in Noah's time. He destroyed everything. But in the ark, God made a way of escape. For us today, that way is Jesus Christ.

Dear God, thank you for sending Jesus Christ to save people in this world.

SAFE IN THE ARK

*"Look! I am about to cover the earth with a flood
that will destroy every living thing. Everything on earth will die!
But I solemnly swear to keep you safe in the boat,
with your wife and your sons and their wives."*
GENESIS 6:17–18 NLT

Have you ever seen a picture of Noah leading animals into the ark? This may be the most pictured event in the Bible. You've probably seen it in books. It is also on puzzles, posters, wallpaper, blankets, curtains, and bed sheets. There are Noah's ark mobiles to hang in baby cribs. There are Noah's ark plush toys to line up on your bed. Could there be any child in America who hasn't seen a picture of Noah's ark?

It is good that people see pictures of Noah and the ark. Noah is usually shown with a long white beard. His wife is at his side, and they both wear long robes. Animals line up in twos, waiting to go into the ark. Usually giraffes, elephants, and lions are there along with some smaller animals. The ark is huge! It looks strong and well built. It has to be so that it can float above God's terrible watery judgment on the earth.

Pictures of Noah's ark remind us that God wants to rescue everyone from judgment. Jesus Christ is like the ark—strong and safe. When you believe in him, it is like entering the ark. In him, you are safe from judgment.

Dear God, thank you for keeping us safe when we believe in you.

WORSHIPING GOD

So Noah, his wife, and his sons and their wives left the boat.
Then Noah built an altar to the LORD.

GENESIS 8:18, 20 NLT

Noah was six hundred years old when he went into the ark to escape the flood. All his family went inside, too. The water in the earth started gushing out everywhere. The sky opened like a window, and rain poured down for forty days and nights. The water became deeper and deeper until the boat could float.

The flood became so deep that even the highest mountains were under water! Not an animal or person was left alive anywhere on the earth. Nothing was alive except Noah and his family and the animals in the ark.

One hundred fifty days later, God made a wind blow. The rain stopped and the flooding stopped. One day the ark came to rest on a mountain. After a while, the other mountaintops could be seen. Finally, the earth was dry. Then God said, "You may now leave the ark." After Noah's family had gone out of the boat, the animals all left, too.

What a terrible time that must have been! And when it was all over, what was the first thing Noah did? He worshiped God. Noah is your example. He teaches you that no matter what happens, remember to worship God.

Dear God, help me to remember to worship you—no matter what happens in my life.

CHANGE OF SEASONS

"Never again will I curse the ground because of man. . . .
As long as the earth endures,
seedtime and harvest, cold and heat, summer and winter,
day and night will never cease."
GENESIS 8:21–22 NIV

When the first day of school comes, the summer is ending. Soon, autumn begins. The weather starts to change as the days become cool. There is less daylight, too. In the morning, the sun rises later, and it sets earlier in the evening. In late October, the nights turn downright frosty! Then comes Thanksgiving Day, and winter is not far ahead.

After Christmas and New Year's Day, winter really hits. Days are darker because the nights are long. In some places, like Oregon, the rains set in. Elsewhere, like in New England, snow falls again and again.

But no matter how long winter seems to be, eventually the snow melts, and the earth dries. Early spring arrives in rivulets of water running in the road. A little bit of green appears here and there. Then one day, the trees show their buds. Suddenly birds sing and leaves are everywhere. Warmth is in the air with the roar of lawn-mowers. Then school is out and summer is back!

When you notice the change of seasons, remember God's promise: "Never again will I curse the ground because of man. . . . As long as the earth endures, seedtime and harvest, cold and heat, summer and winter, day and night will never cease."

Dear God, thank you for our earth and all its beautiful seasons.

THE RAINBOW'S PROMISE

*And God said, "I am giving you a sign. . . . I have placed my rainbow in the clouds.
. . . Never again will there be a flood that will destroy all life."*
GENESIS 9:12–13, 15 NLT

Do you like to see rainbows in the sky? They are so beautiful! Do
you know what makes a rainbow? Sun shining through falling rain.
But in Noah's time, there had never been a rainbow before. The
rains that brought the flood were the first rains ever. When Noah
saw the rains ending, the sun came out. Then Noah and his family
saw the very first rainbow ever, and
they knew they had survived the
Great Flood.

Imagine what Noah's family
felt the next time rain clouds came.
They must have been afraid of the
rain. After all, the first time it
rained, the flood destroyed the
whole earth! But God didn't want
them to be afraid. God promised
Noah and his family that he would
never again destroy the earth with
a flood. Rainbows are a reminder
that this promise is true. God has kept this promise to Noah. Since
the time of Noah, floods have never destroyed the whole earth.
Remember this whenever you see a rainbow.

The Bible tells many of God's promises. All these are as real and
beautiful as a rainbow. And all of them are true!

Dear God, thank you for always keeping your word!

THE TOWER OF BABEL

So the LORD scattered them from there over all the earth,
and they stopped building the city.
GENESIS 11:8 NIV

The people of Babel all spoke the same language. This is why they thought they could build that huge tower. Imagine a tower reaching to heaven! If they could do this, they could do anything. Whatever they did, they would do it without God.

God came to see what was happening in Babel. He saw the beginning of the tower and the city of Babel. He saw all the people, far from him and his ways. All the people spoke the same language, so God knew they could do anything they wanted. But whatever they did, it would be godless, lifeless, built of brick.

So God confused their language. Suddenly people could not understand each other. How could they make bricks or build with them? They couldn't do this anymore. It was the end of Babel. The people scattered from there all over the earth. They finally did what God asked them to do after the flood—they filled the earth.

Since then, the nations of the earth have never come together to build. The day will come, though, when the nations gather again. That is the day of the second coming of Jesus!

Dear God, help me never to do anything without you.

ABRAHAM

The Lord told Abram,
"Leave your country, your relatives, and your father's house,
and go to the land that I will show you. . . . I will bless you."
GENESIS 12:1–2 NLT

A man named Abraham lived not far from that old city of Babel. His hometown was named Ur in the land that is now called Iraq.

One day, God appeared to Abraham there and said, "Get out of your country and leave your relatives, and come to a land that I will show you."

Imagine that you're Abraham. You're in the town where you were born. Your family and friends all live there. The streets and shops are all familiar to you. You like it there. Then God appears to you and speaks to you: "Leave here. Leave everything you know, all your friends and your family. I will lead you to another place far away."

Would you be able to do this? Could you go all alone to a place you'd never even heard of? Abraham did this. Don't you wonder why?

Here's why: It is hard to resist God. He is everything that we need. And he blesses us when we obey him. This is why Abraham followed God. And this is why many others have done the same thing.

Dear God, help me obey you.

DRAWN TO GOD

There he built an altar and worshiped the LORD.
GENESIS 12:8 NLT

Abraham was seventy-five years old when he crossed into the new land. His wife, Sarah, and his nephew, Lot, were with him. God had led Abraham to the land called Canaan. One day this little group was camping beside a big oak tree. The Lord came to Abraham there. God said, "I'm going to give this land to your children."

What did Abraham do when he was told of this amazing gift? He built an altar. He wanted to worship God.

From the oak tree, Abraham moved to Bethel. There he built another altar to worship the Lord. By this time, Abraham loved God very much. He knew how beautiful God is. He'd heard God's voice and knew there is nothing to fear in God. God held him like a big refrigerator holds a little magnet. Abraham couldn't get away from God. He didn't want to. This is why people worship God.

The way Abraham worshiped is the way you can worship. This is the first way a man ever worshiped. He called on the name of the Lord. It is so simple. Anyone can worship this way. With love, say, "Lord Jesus." God hears you. This is worship.

Dear God, help me to worship you all the time.

A BIG FAMILY

Abram believed the LORD, and he credited it to him as righteousness.
GENESIS 15:6 NIV

Abraham was with God one night looking up at the starry sky. There God made a promise to Abraham. Imagine them talking to each other like this:

"Can you count the stars, Abraham?" asked God.

"No, of course not."

Then God said to Abraham, "You and Sarah are going to have as many children as the stars."

Abraham was stunned. He could say nothing. He may have thought, *That is amazing—as many children as the stars in the sky!*

In the silence, Abraham gazed at the stars and considered what God had said. Finally, he said, "I believe you."

These might be the most important words ever spoken. Abraham was the first person to believe in God. This is why he is called the father of faith. Faith in God began with him. Not only so, Abraham and Sarah did have a child. When they were very old, Isaac was born. Isaac's son was named Jacob. He is sometimes called Israel. The Bible tells the story of the children of Israel. These are the people of the Jewish faith. God's promise was true because Abraham's children are too many to be counted!

Dear God, thank you that I can believe in you!

FEASTING WITH GOD

The LORD appeared again to Abraham while he was camped
near the oak grove belonging to Mamre.
GENESIS 18:1 NLT

One day God and two angels came into Abraham's camp. Abraham was honored to welcome them. He said, "Let me make some food to refresh you. Please stay awhile before you go on your way."

"All right," said God and the angels.

As the three sat in the shade of an oak tree, Abraham and Sarah cooked a meal. Sarah baked some bread while Abraham ran out to his herd and chose a fat calf. He killed it and roasted the meat. When this was ready, he took the meat and bread with cheese and milk and served it to the men.

This is the first time a person ever feasted with God. In time, people learned that God likes this. He enjoys feasting with us. From the time of Abraham to the time of Jesus, worship and food went together.

This is still true today. But we don't bake bread and roast meat to feast with God. We have Jesus. He said, "I am the bread of life." When you sing and pray to God, you eat the bread of life. Jesus Christ is food for your soul and for your spirit.

Dear God, thank you for giving me the bread of life—Jesus!

NOTHING IS TOO HARD

"Is anything too hard for the LORD?"
GENESIS 18:14 NLT

In the shade of the oaks at Mamre, God ate lunch with Abraham. As they were eating, God said, ""Where is Sarah, your wife?"

"In the tent," Abraham replied.

Then God said, "About this time next year I'll return. Then your wife Sarah will have a son."

God had made this promise before. But this time Sarah was listening through the thin walls of her tent. She laughed silently to herself when she heard it. "How could a worn-out old woman like me have a baby?" she thought. "And my husband is so old!"

Even though Sarah's laugh was silent, God heard it.

"Why did Sarah laugh?" the Lord asked. "Why did she say, 'Can an old woman like me have a baby?'"

Sarah was afraid. "I didn't laugh," she lied.

But God said, "That is not true. You did laugh."

God has made many promises, and they are all written in the Bible. Some people, like Sarah, find these promises hard to believe. But God taught her, saying, "Is anything too hard for the Lord?" Sarah knew the answer to this question—no!

Then, God promised again, "In a year, just as I told you, I will return. Sarah will have a son."

Dear God, help me to remember that nothing is too hard for you!

PROMISES KEPT

Now the Lord was gracious to Sarah as he had said,
and the Lord did for Sarah what he had promised.
GENESIS 21:1 NIV

God said to Abraham, "I will bless Sarah. She'll give birth to your son. Yes, I will richly bless her. She will become the mother of many nations."

When Abraham heard this, he bowed down to worship God.

But at the same time, he laughed silently. Even the father of faith didn't believe this could happen. "How could I become a father at the age of one hundred?" he wondered. "Besides, Sarah is ninety. How could she have a baby?"

Then the Lord did exactly what was promised. Sarah became pregnant and she and Abraham had a son. It all happened when God had said it would. Abraham was one hundred years old at the time. He named his son Isaac. That name means, "He laughs."

Sarah was so happy! She said, "God has brought me laughter! Everybody who hears about this will laugh with me. Who would have dreamed that I would ever have a baby? Yet I have given Abraham a son in his old age!"

God has made many promises to us. When Jesus came, he proved all the promises to be true. This is why, when we worship God, we say "amen." This means, "It is true."

Dear God, thank you for proving that all your promises are true.

SACRIFICE

*Then God said, "Take your son, your only son, Isaac, whom you love,
and go to the region of Moriah. Sacrifice him there as a burnt offering."*
GENESIS 22:2 NIV

All his life, old Abraham had no children. Then, when he was one
hundred years old, God gave him a son. Isaac was a precious treasure
to Abraham. Think about how Abraham must have loved his son.

One day God told Abraham, "Take your only son; take Isaac,
whom you love so much, and sacrifice him." The word *sacrifice*
means to give up something pre-
cious. God asked Abraham to kill
Isaac! Why would God do this?

Abraham loved and trusted
God more than anything or anyone else. What did he think about
as he walked to the mountain to
sacrifice Isaac? He remembered
God's promise from long before
Isaac was born. "Look up at the
night sky and count the stars if you
can," God said. "Your children will
be like that—too many to count!"

He thought of his wife, Sarah. It was impossible for her to have a
baby. Yet, she'd had the baby Isaac. Abraham didn't think that God
was wrong to ask for a sacrifice.

Old Abraham trusted God and went to sacrifice his son. He
understood that if Isaac died, God could bring him back to life
again. And in a way, that is just what happened!

*Dear God, help me to remember all that you have done for me. Thank you that I can
trust in you.*

ETERNAL LIFE

He went over and took the ram and sacrificed it
as a burnt offering instead of his son.
GENESIS 22:13 NIV

Abraham, the man of faith, was about to kill his only son! But suddenly something happened that had happened once before. God provided an animal to die instead. Remember when Adam and Eve ate from the wrong tree? They were supposed to die because of their sin. Instead, God killed a lamb and covered their nakedness.

God showed Abraham a ram caught in a bramble, and he sacrificed the ram instead of Isaac.

Both of these stories show us what God did when he sent his  Son. Jesus Christ came to save us from sin. This sin came when Adam disobeyed God. God loves the world and wants to be close to us like a Father. So he sent us Jesus. Some people called him the Lamb of God. This is not because he was gentle and lovely to look at. Jesus is the Lamb of God because he died for our sin. He was like the ram in the story of Abraham and Isaac. He died so that we can live with God.

Jesus himself explained this in the best way. "God so loved the world that he gave his only Son. Everyone who believes in him will not perish but have eternal life."

Dear God, thank you for providing Jesus to save me from my sin.

THE BIRTHRIGHT

So Jacob insisted, "Well then, swear to me right now that it is mine."
So Esau swore an oath. . . .selling all his rights
as the firstborn to his younger brother.
GENESIS 25:33 NLT

Esau and Jacob were brothers, the twin sons of Isaac. The two were not alike at all. Esau was a hunter who loved to be in the woods and fields. Jacob was a quiet man who liked to stay at home. One day Jacob was simmering a pot of soup over the fire. Esau came home and begged his brother for some soup. He must not have eaten all day because he was starving. Jacob said, "I'll trade you some soup for your birthright."

What is a birthright? It is what someone is given when his or her parents die. It could be a house, some land, or money. A birthright could be something small but very important to the family. For example, I will be given something wonderful that belonged to my great-grandfather.

Esau traded his birthright to Jacob for a bowl of soup. This means that he didn't care for his family. Esau's birthright was the land that God promised to his grandfather Abraham. But Esau was hungry for something else and gave up his family's land.

This story teaches about your family and mine. We may not be rich like Abraham and Jacob. But our families are precious. Let's not trade them for anything!

Dear God, thank you for my family.

THE WRESTLING MATCH

"Your name will no longer be Jacob,"
"but Israel, because you have struggled with God
and with men and have overcome."
GENESIS 32:28 NIV

Jacob was alone, praying by the Jabbok River. While he was praying, a man came and wrestled with him until dawn. Finally, the man saw that he couldn't win the wrestling match. So, he hit Jacob in the hip and knocked it out of joint.

The man said, "Let me go. It's dawn."

Jacob was out of breath, "I will not let you go unless you bless me," he said.

"What's your name?" the man asked.

"Jacob," he replied.

"Your name isn't Jacob anymore," the man told him. "It is now Israel. You have struggled with both God and men and have won." Then he blessed Jacob.

This story tells us a lot. One simple thing to remember about it is this: Prayer can change you. After this night of prayer, Jacob was always called Israel. His name changed. And, he limped for the rest of his life. Prayer even changed the way he walked through this world!

But we don't have to wrestle all night in prayer with God, although we could. The simplest little prayer can change you. Just say, "Jesus, I love you," and your life will be different!

Dear God, I love you.

FAVORITE SON

But his brothers hated Joseph because of their father's partiality.
They couldn't say a kind word to him.
GENESIS 37:4 NLT

Jacob had twelve sons. The youngest was the son of Rachel, and Jacob loved him dearly. His name was Joseph. Jacob loved Joseph more than he loved his brothers. This was a mistake.

Jacob showed his love by dressing Joseph better than the rest of his children. He gave him a beautiful coat. He probably did other special things for the boy, too. This was Jacob's mistake. Parents should not love one of their children more than they do another. When this happens, children soon take notice of it. It can cause fights and quarrels in families. This is why his brothers hated Joseph. They even wanted to kill him!

But remember that this is the story of a family. Bad feelings can come up in families. People can do things and say things that they shouldn't. Jacob shouldn't have loved Joseph more than he loved his other eleven sons, but he did. Not only did this hurt the others, it hurt Joseph most. His brothers couldn't even say a nice word to him. Imagine how hard that was for young Joseph!

But, as we shall see, God had a purpose for this troubled family.

Dear God, thank you for having a purpose for me, even in hard times.

NEVER ALONE

When Joseph arrived, they pulled off his beautiful robe and threw him into the pit.
GENESIS 37:23–24 NLT

Joseph was in a deep, dry pit without his beautiful coat. How could such a thing happen? He was the great-grandson of Abraham, the father of faith. When Abraham was in a faraway land, God had come to him. Abraham had followed God to a new land and God gave it to him. Many years later, Joseph was trapped in a hole in the ground of that same land.

Many times, God told Abraham he would be blessed. And

 Abraham was the first person to believe in God. Abraham's son Isaac also believed God for the blessings. Isaac's son Jacob wrestled with God for those blessings. But could this be a blessing? Jacob's sons stripped the clothes from their father's beloved son. They threw him in a pit in the ground and left him to die. But along came some traders, and Joseph's brothers sold him to the traders for twenty pieces of silver. The boy was taken to Egypt and sold as a slave.

Certainly, Jacob told Joseph about the night he'd wrestled with God. Joseph knew of God's promised blessings. He'd heard about his grandfather's wonderful birth. Abraham's journeys were his bedtime stories. So Joseph wasn't alone in Egypt. He lived with God's promises.

Dear God, help me to remember your promises, especially during hard times.

GOD'S BLESSINGS

*Joseph was thirty years old when he entered
the service of Pharaoh king of Egypt.*
GENESIS 41:46 NIV

As it happened, Joseph grew up to be the wisest man in Egypt. He was filled with the spirit of God. This is why he became the assistant to Egypt's king, called Pharaoh. Joseph was in charge of Pharaoh's household and of all Egypt. Pharaoh put his own ring on Joseph's finger. He dressed him in beautiful clothing and placed the royal gold chain around his neck. Pharaoh also gave Joseph a chariot so he could travel around the land. He said, "No one will even move in my country without Joseph's permission."

All this was much better than one coat of many colors. Joseph was dressed in the best clothes in all of Egypt! He was in charge of the richest country in the world!

Two sons were born to him and his wife, Asenath. The older son was named Manasseh. This name means, "God has made me forget my troubles and my father's family." Joseph named his second son Ephraim. This means, "God has blessed me in the land of my suffering." The names of Joseph's sons mean a lot. They show that Joseph didn't forget God. And so, God's promised blessings came to Joseph.

Dear God, thank you for your many blessings.

GOOD FROM EVIL

Now Joseph was the governor of the land,
the one who sold grain to all its people.
So when Joseph's brothers arrived,
they bowed down to him with their faces to the ground.
GENESIS 42:6 NIV

Time passed. Famine came to that part of the world. When there is famine, no food can grow. But Joseph was wise and filled with the Spirit of God. He had stored up enough food for all the people in Egypt. Even people from other places came to buy food from Joseph.

Joseph's brothers had no idea what had happened to their brother. They hadn't seen him since they sold him many years before. Like everyone else, they came to buy food from Joseph. First, all the brothers except Benjamin went to Egypt. Later, Benjamin and Jacob came, too. So the whole family was there. But they didn't know Joseph was selling them food. Joseph had lived in Egypt for so long that his family didn't recognize him! Then he finally told his family who he was. He wept so loud that his crying was heard all around the palace.

God didn't forget the promises when Joseph came to Egypt. Here is what he said to his brothers: "God sent me here to keep you and your families alive. Now you will become a great nation, as he promised. Yes, God sent me here, not you!"

Dear God, thank you for turning bad situations into good ones.

LIFE IS SHORT

Joseph brought his father Jacob in and presented him before Pharaoh.
After Jacob blessed Pharaoh, Pharaoh asked him, "How old are you?"
GENESIS 47:7–8 NIV

Joseph loved, honored, and respected his father, so he introduced him to Pharaoh. This most powerful man in the world asked Jacob a common question, "How old are you?" Jacob was an old man who had lived a hard life. It was right for Pharaoh to admire him.

Jacob counted the length of his life in days. But a day is short, it ends quickly. Yet, we can live only one day at a time. All our days add up to a lifetime. Even though Jacob had lived for 130 years, he said his days were few. This means that life just doesn't last long enough.

Jacob told Pharaoh that his life was a pilgrimage. This is a journey or a trip to someplace very special. He saw himself as a stranger in this world. He was traveling to his real home in God. This earth was like a hotel to Jacob. It was not his home. This is true of all people who have come to know God as Jacob did. We are sojourners. That means we are not here to stay. We will only live a short time and then spend forever with God in heaven!

Dear God, thank you for heaven where we will live forever with you.

PASS-ALONG PROMISES

When Jacob was told, "Your son Joseph has come to you,"
Israel rallied his strength and sat up on the bed.
Jacob said to Joseph, "God Almighty appeared to me at Luz
in the land of Canaan, and there he blessed me."
GENESIS 48:2—3 NIV

By this time, there had been three generations of God's believers.
Abraham and Sarah were the first people to believe God's promises.
Their son, Isaac, married Rebekah. They also followed God and
hoped in the promises. Esau sold his birthright to Jacob for a bowl
of soup. So Jacob and his wives, Leah and Rachel, were the third
generation. They lived by faith in God, too.

When Jacob was dying, he called Joseph to his deathbed.
There he repeated God's promises. The family was in Egypt,
which was far away from the land that God promised to them. But
the promises were still true. They were the same promises that
Abraham first believed. God gave them to Isaac and later to Jacob.
Here God didn't speak the promises directly to Joseph. Instead,
Joseph's father Jacob spoke for God. The son heard the gospel
from his father.

Today, God's promises are passed along this same way, like food
at Thanksgiving. The food is passed around the table. Each person
takes some and passes the dish to the next person. This is how
God's promises in Christ are made known.

Dear God, thank you for giving me others to tell me about your promises. Help me
to tell others, too.

GOING HOME

"I am about to be gathered to my people.
Bury me with my fathers."
GENESIS 49:29 NIV

Have you seen the movie *The Wizard of Oz*? It is the exciting story of Dorothy and her dog, Toto. A tornado whirled through Kansas and carried them far away. After many adventures, it came time for them to return to Kansas. Dorothy said good-bye to Scarecrow and Lion. Then she tapped the heels of her ruby slippers together three times. At the same time she said, "There's no place like home. There's no place like home." And then she was home again.

When Jacob died in Egypt, he wanted to go home. His parents, grandparents, and wife, Leah, were buried in the land of Canaan. God gave this land to them. But Jacob also wanted his children to remember that land. They had been away from it for seventeen years. But they had to return to bury their father. This caused them to remember God's promise to give them that land.

Still today, we remember the gospel's promise when someone dies. Jesus said, ""I am the resurrection and the life. Those who believe in me, even though they die like everyone else, will live again."

Dear God, thank you that there is no place like our home in heaven.

FORGIVENESS

Then his brothers came and bowed low before him.
"We are your slaves," they said.
But Joseph told them, "Don't be afraid of me. Am I God,
to judge and punish you?
Indeed, I myself will take care of you and your families."
GENESIS 50:18–19, 21 NLT

When I was a boy, I had many animals as pets. I had pigeons, turtles, lizards, dogs, ducks, rabbits, and chickens. One day I went out

to my chicken coop and saw that a stray dog had killed my chickens. I took a stick and hit that dog as hard as I could. He yelped and ran away. Later I felt bad about hitting the dog. He didn't know it was wrong to kill those birds. It was natural for him to do it. The next time I saw the dog, I said, "I'm sorry that I hurt you." I knew that the dog didn't understand me, but my apology made me feel better.

When they were young, Joseph's brothers abused him. They stripped the clothes off of him and dumped him in a deep hole and left him there to die. But they saw they could make money if they sold him to some traders. So Joseph was carried to Egypt to become a slave.

I wonder when Joseph's brothers began to feel bad about what they had done. What a weight to carry all your life. It must have felt so good to apologize. Imagine their peace when he forgave and comforted them.

Dear God, thank you for forgiveness.

THE JOURNEY

Then Joseph said to his brothers, "I am about to die.
But God will surely come to your aid and take you up out of this land
to the land he promised on oath to Abraham, Isaac and Jacob."
GENESIS 50:24 NIV

Didn't the book of Genesis begin wonderfully? In the Garden of Eden, Adam and Eve had everything they could ever want. But Genesis ends far, far from that garden. It ends with the body of Joseph in a coffin in Egypt.

It was a long journey from Eden to Egypt. The people of the garden left God. They traveled through pain, sweat, and murder. Yet, God followed them in love with promises along the way. God told them unforgettable things about a good land to live in. They believed God. Their family would have as many members as there are stars in the sky.

Yes, Genesis ends with Joseph's body in a coffin. But that coffin is not buried in Egypt. Joseph's faith in God's promises wouldn't allow this. The people had a long way to go on their journey. Joseph made sure they would take his bones and God's promises with them. "God will come for you," Joseph told his brothers. "You will leave this land of Egypt. The Lord will bring you back to live in the Promised Land. This is God's pledge to your fathers Abraham, Isaac, and Jacob."

Dear God, thank you for loving me even when I'm not going the right way.

HARD TIMES

Then a new king came to the throne of Egypt
who knew nothing about Joseph or what he had done.
He told his people, "These Israelites are becoming a threat
to us because there are so many of them."
EXODUS 1:8—9 NLT

The children of Israel had a good thing going in Egypt. Because of Joseph, the Pharaohs liked them. This is why they lived in Goshen, which was good land near the sea. In time, Joseph and each of his brothers died. But they had many children and grandchildren. In fact, there were so many of them that they soon filled the land. This happened because of God's promise to Abraham, Isaac, and Jacob. Sure enough, God's promise was true. They had a huge family.

Remember when God told Abraham to leave his hometown? That was when God first told Abraham his family would be a great nation. And God's promised blessing came. After 430 years, some people think there were at least 600,000 Israelites living in Egypt!

Then something frightening happened. Here's what the Bible says: "A new king came to the throne of Egypt. He knew nothing about Joseph or what he had done." This means that things were about to change for the worse. You and your family may believe in God just like the Israelites. But change can bring hard times. God's promises won't protect you from change, but he will help you through it.

Dear God, thank you for helping me through change and hard times.

GOD NEVER CHANGES

They were ruthless with the Israelites, forcing them to make bricks
and mortar and to work long hours in the fields.
EXODUS 1:14 NLT

Pharaoh was worried because there were so many Israelites. "We must put an end to this," he said. "If we don't and if war breaks out, they will fight against us."

So the Egyptians made the Israelites their slaves. Brutal slave drivers tried to wear them down with hard work. They forced them to build cities for the king. But this didn't stop the Israelites from having more children. So the frightened Egyptians made their slavery even worse. The Israelites were cruelly forced to make bricks and work long hours in the fields.

The history of Israel is big and important. By it, we can understand what it means to have faith in God. For us today, just like Israel long ago, things always change. They don't always get worse, but they always change. But God doesn't change. The Bible says, "In ages past, you laid the foundation of the earth, and the heavens are the work of your hands. . .they will wear out like old clothing. You will change them like a garment, and they will fade away. But you are always the same; your years never end."

Dear God, thank you for always staying the same, even when my life is changing.

EVIL PLANS

Then Pharaoh gave this order to all his people:
"Every boy that is born you must throw into the river,
but let every girl live."
EXODUS 1:22 NIV

Pharaoh only needed the Israelites to serve him. But the Egyptians made them serve with *rigor*. This means that their work was harsh, strict, and never-ending. The Egyptians wanted the Israelites' lives to be terrible. They wanted to break their spirits and rob them of their humanity. Such work would ruin their health, and they would die. Then there would be fewer Israelites. The Egyptians probably hoped that slavery would stop the Israelites from marrying and having more children. Who would want their children to be born into slavery?

Pharaoh wanted to put an end to Israel, but his plans did not work. Israel got stronger, so the Egyptians turned to something horrible—they began to murder the Israelites' children.

Those ancient people were very evil, but no matter what they did, the Egyptians couldn't stop God's purpose. As the Bible says, "The rulers plot together against the Lord. . . . But the one who rules in heaven laughs. The Lord scoffs at them."

Dear God, thank you for your loving power.

A BABY in A BASKET

But when she could hide him no longer, she got a papyrus basket for him
and coated it with tar and pitch.
Then she placed the child in it and put it among
the reeds along the bank of the Nile.
EXODUS 2:3 NIV

Think of it. Pharaoh wanted to destroy Israel. He was ruthless about it. The Israelites spent long days working for him like slaves. Pharaoh then decided to kill every Israelite baby boy that was born. Fear must have filled the hearts and homes of the Israelites. In one of those homes a boy was born, and his parents hid him from the Egyptians for three months. One day they decided that they couldn't hide him anymore. They wove a basket out of reeds and made it waterproof with tar. The mother put her child in it and carried it to the river. She left it floating there, hidden by the reeds.

She wept as she walked away, leaving her little boy alone. *What will happen to him? Will he starve to death? Will he float away on the tide, down the river and into the sea? A crocodile could eat him! Will someone rescue him?* The mother prayed for her little boy. Only God could save him.

She didn't know that this was a new beginning for Israel. "God will come for you," Joseph had told his brothers. "You will leave this land of Egypt." And God used a baby in a basket to do this.

Dear God, help me to remember that you can do anything!

MOSES

Then Pharaoh's daughter. . .saw the basket among the reeds
and sent her slave girl to get it. She opened it and saw the baby.
He was crying, and she felt sorry for him.
EXODUS 2:5–6 NIV

God cared tenderly for Israel in this way. Someone came to bathe at the riverside that day. This was the only person in the world who could save the little boy. It was Pharaoh's daughter. God guided her to the place where the baby's basket floated. She heard him cry and rescued him.

The wonders didn't stop there. Pharaoh's daughter hired the baby's own mother as his nurse. The mother, father, and son were to-

gether until he grew up. So the boy learned all about God's promises to Israel. Growing up he heard about Abraham, Isaac, and Jacob. He knew about the Promised Land that God had given them. He understood God's promise that Israel would become a great nation. He could never forget the words of Joseph: "God will come for you. You will leave this land of Egypt. The Lord will bring you back to live in the Promised Land. This is God's pledge to your fathers Abraham, Isaac, and Jacob."

He was twelve or thirteen years old when he went to the palace. There he lived with Pharaoh's daughter and learned all the ways of the Egyptians. And Pharaoh's daughter named him Moses.

Dear God, thank you for caring for your people.

GOD'S WORK

When Moses had grown up, he went out to visit his people,
the Israelites, and he saw how hard they were forced to work.
During his visit, he saw an Egyptian beating one of the Hebrew slaves.
After looking around to make sure no one was watching,
Moses killed the Egyptian and buried him in the sand.

EXODUS 2:11–12 NLT

Moses was the best man to save Israel from slavery. His Hebrew mother and father raised him. This means he knew all about the Israelites. He knew where they came from and where they were going. Then, Pharaoh's family adopted Moses. So he was trained in all the ways and wisdom of the Egyptians.

But Moses still had something to learn. He didn't know God yet. When he killed an Egyptian for hitting a Hebrew, he made a mistake. Yes, it was wrong to kill the man, but there is something more. Moses' mistake was that he thought he could save Israel by himself. No matter how God prepared him, he could not do this.

Maybe Moses forgot that Joseph said, "*God* will come for you." How was it possible for the Lord to bring them back to the Promised Land? Moses couldn't understand this. So he tried to do it himself. He was a smart man with a good education. But he was a big failure at the one thing he really wanted to do. He couldn't save Israel. Soon he would learn that only God could do God's work.

Dear God, thank you for doing your work.

NEVER FORGET

Moses fled from Pharaoh and escaped to the land of Midian.
EXODUS 2:15 NLT

Moses ran away. He had to run because Pharaoh wanted to kill him. After all, he had murdered a man. He went all the way to a place called Midian. There he met the seven daughters of a shepherd named Reuel. This man welcomed him, and Moses married one of his daughters. Her name was Zipporah. Together they had a son named Gershom, which means, "I am a stranger in a strange land."

Do you think that Moses was lonely? In Egypt, everyone knew him, both the Hebrews and the Egyptian royal family. He could do anything and go anywhere. But then he had to run far away into the wilderness. There he became a shepherd for his wife's father's sheep. What else could he do? He had no sheep of his own. He was a stranger in a strange land.

From birth until the day he ran away, Moses lived forty years in Egypt. There he was famous. He spent forty more years herding sheep in the wilderness. He thought he'd been forgotten. But in all those years, Moses didn't forget his people Israel. God didn't forget them, either. Even if they forget him, God never forgets the people he loves.

Dear God, thank you for never forgetting me.

PRAYER CHANGES THINGS

The Israelites groaned in their slavery and cried out,
and their cry for help because of their slavery went up to God.
God heard their groaning and he remembered his covenant with Abraham,
with Isaac and with Jacob. So God looked on the Israelites
and was concerned about them.

EXODUS 2:23–25 NIV

Do you know when people usually pray to God? When they are in trouble. It is best to pray because of love for God. But usually it isn't that way. Israel's story shows us this is true.

Egypt probably stopped murdering the Hebrew children. After all, the people of Israel were their slaves. Pharaoh was content with this. The people just continued to work, year after year. One Pharaoh died and another one took his place. Each was as cruel as the one before. People were born, people died, and Israel's work was harsh, strict, and never-ending. The Bible doesn't report that they prayed or thought about God. Maybe some wondered why God hadn't come to rescue them, but that's all.

Meanwhile, Moses was on the other side of the wilderness. It was a shame that he was keeping sheep there. Maybe he thought it was better than making bricks in Egypt. He surely never thought about going back to Egypt.

At last, someone in Egypt remembered God and cried out in prayer. People couldn't stand the slavery anymore and prayed. That prayer changed things for Israel and for Moses.

Dear God, help me to pray to you all the time.

THE BURNING BUSH

The angel of the LORD appeared to him in flames of fire from within a bush.
Moses saw that though the bush was on fire it did not burn up.

EXODUS 3:2 NIV

Can you picture a bush that is burning but is not burnt up? This is how Moses first met God. No one can forget this picture. Moses never did. He remembered this bush in his final words. When he

blessed the tribe of Joseph, he mentioned "the one who dwells in the bush." There was nothing special about this bush. The bush was like thousands of bushes on that mountain. The one thing different was that it was burning with God.

In the New Testament God is seen, but not in a bush. God came as an ordinary man—Jesus Christ. There was nothing beautiful about him. Many people didn't pay attention to him. In fact, he was hated.

He was rejected. People looked the other way when he went by.

The story of Moses and the burning bush is miraculous. Even more, it is a reminder of Jesus who came to help us. God lived in this simple man. He was like the burning bush, blazing with God but not burnt up.

Dear God, thank you for working in miraculous ways!

ORDINARY THINGS

God called to him from within the bush, "Moses! Moses!"
And Moses said, "Here I am."
EXODUS 3:4 NIV

Moses was born to bring Israel out of slavery, but nothing happened until he was eighty years old. He spent forty years as a prince in Egypt. The next forty years he was a shepherd in Midian. This was a poor job for a man like him, but he seemed to be happy with it. God used it to teach Moses humility.

Would you like to be a prince in an Egyptian palace? Or would you rather keep sheep alone in a dusty desert? Before you answer, remember one thing: Moses saw more of God in the desert than in all the palaces of Egypt. The Bible teaches that God likes to use the powerless and lowly things. This shames the mighty and the strong. That is what happened to Moses. There was a humble old shepherd and an ordinary bush. But God began to burn in them, and the world changed!

Dear God, thank you for using the ordinary to do the extraordinary!

COME CLOSE TO GOD

Then the LORD told him, "You can be sure I have seen the misery of my people
in Egypt. . . . So I have come to rescue them from the Egyptians
and lead them out of Egypt. . . . Now go, for I am sending you to Pharaoh.
You will lead my people, the Israelites, out of Egypt."
EXODUS 3:7–8, 10 NLT

Moses could have passed by the burning bush. Maybe it was a hot day. Who would want to be by a fire then? But Moses stopped to look. Here's how the Bible describes it:

"Amazing!" Moses said to himself. "Why isn't that bush burning up? I must go over to see this." When the Lord saw that he had caught Moses' attention, God called to him from the bush, "Moses! Moses!"

"Here I am!" Moses replied.

We were made to seek God as if we were feeling around in the dark. And we are meant to find God. Moses had been with sheep in the desert for forty years. Yet, he was still seeking God. This is why he said, "I must go over and see this." If he hadn't done this, God would have let him pass by. Only when he turned to see the bush did God call to him. The Bible teaches that we first must come close to God. We must seek God. Then God will come close to us. That is what happened to Moses.

God said to Moses, "I am sending you to Pharaoh. You will lead my people, the Israelites, out of Egypt." Just imagine Moses' surprise!

Dear God, draw me close to you in amazing ways.

IT'S NOT ABOUT ME

*"But who am I to appear before Pharaoh?" Moses asked God.
"How can you expect me to lead the Israelites out of Egypt?"
Then God told him, "I will be with you."*

EXODUS 3:11–12 NLT

"Who am I," asked Moses, "that I should go to Pharaoh, and that I should bring the children of Israel out of Egypt?" This is a very good question. Moses already knew who he was—the adopted son of Pharaoh's daughter. He was also a murderer who, decades earlier, had fled from Egypt. He knew he was married to the daughter of the priest of Midian. How could he forget that he was nothing but a shepherd? He himself said, "I am a stranger in a strange land."

Moses was surprised that God would tell him, "I will send you to Pharaoh to bring my people, the Israelites, out of Egypt."

Moses knew he couldn't do this. Forty years of herding sheep had taught him this. So he asked, "Who am I that I should go to Pharaoh?"

This was the wrong question. As you grow up in the Lord, try not to look at yourself. Jesus is the one to look at. The question isn't, "Who am I?" It is, "Who are *you*, Lord?" God loves to answer this question.

And God said to Moses, "Certainly I will be with you."

Dear God, help me to look at you, not at myself.

WHO GOD IS

Moses said to God, "Suppose I go to the Israelites and say to them,
'The God of your fathers has sent me to you,' and they ask me,
'What is his name?' Then what shall I tell them?"
God said to Moses, "I am who I am."

EXODUS 3:13–14 NIV

Everything has a name and when you hear a name, you know what it is. A desk is a desk. A chair is a chair. You know what to think of when you hear the word *dog*. The word *cat* makes you think of a cat. But what does the name *I am who I am* mean? This is hard to explain because it is God's name. God is a mystery. We only know a little bit about God.

I'll tell you what I know about God's name. The name *I am who I am* tells that God does not depend on anyone or anything. Children depend on their parents. A wife depends on her husband. A husband depends on his wife. But God depends on no one. He is independent of everything. The name also means that everything depends on God. The source of all life is God. The beginning and end of everything is God.

Who is God? You must be satisfied to know that God is who God is. This is who God always was and ever will be.

Dear God, thank you for being who you are.

THE NAME

God also said to Moses, "Say to the Israelites,
'The LORD, the God of your fathers—the God of Abraham,
the God of Isaac and the God of Jacob—has sent me to you.'
This is my name forever, the name by which I am to be remembered
from generation to generation."
EXODUS 3:15 NIV

The name *I am who I am* might puzzle the children of Israel. So Moses was given another name of God. This one is more familiar. "The Lord God of your fathers has sent me to you." This is the God of Abraham, Isaac, and Jacob. This name would bring faith to life in the enslaved Hebrews. Their memories of God's promises had grown dim, but Moses would bring the name of the God of their fathers.

This name would bring to mind old Abraham and his wife, Sarah. The Hebrews would remember that this old couple could have no children. But their faith in God's Word was enough for Isaac to be born.

When Moses brought this name, someone would begin to tell stories. "Remember that faithful Abraham was going to sacrifice Isaac? But God sent a ram to be killed instead." Then the story of Jacob wrestling with God would be told. Each story would include God's promise of the Promised Land and of a great nation of Israel.

Israel would be strengthened to know that this is God's name forever. It is an eternal memorial to God's faithfulness to his chosen people.

Dear God, thank you for your wonderful name.

IT'S A MIRACLE!

*Moses reached out and took hold of the snake
and it turned back into a staff in his hand.
"This," said the LORD, "is so that they may believe that the LORD,
the God of their fathers—the God of Abraham,
the God of Isaac and the God of Jacob—has appeared to you."*
EXODUS 4:4–5 NIV

When I was a boy, I had a deck of trick playing cards. I could do magical things with those cards. Cards would appear in the deck where they shouldn't have been. I could shuffle them in the same order repeatedly. I called this magic. But it was all a trick. Some of the cards were a little shorter than the others. That was the trick. I also practiced a lot, just like a magician has to practice many hours to pull a rabbit from his hat.

Moses' wooden staff turned into a snake. Then he picked up the snake and it was a staff again. This wasn't a trick. It wasn't magic. It was a miracle! Moses hadn't practiced. He didn't say magic words. He just threw his staff on the ground and it turned into a snake. Moses was so surprised at this that he ran from it.

Miracles come only from God and only at special times. Moses would soon go to Egypt where God would change the world. The miracles that went along with this came from God. They showed the people that they were seeing the work of God.

Dear God, thank you for your miracles.

HEALED FROM SIN

Then the LORD said to Moses, "Put your hand inside your robe."
Moses did so, and when he took it out again,
his hand was white as snow with leprosy.
"Now put your hand back into your robe again,"
the LORD said. Moses did, and when he took it out this time,
it was as healthy as the rest of his body.
EXODUS 4:6–7 NLT

God sends miracles to help people believe in him. Moses was afraid that the Israelites wouldn't believe that God sent him. So God showed Moses the miracles that the people would see. Moses didn't work miracles by his own power. Nor did he do them for people's praise. The miracles came from God for God's glory.

Moses put his hand under his shirt by his heart. He pulled it out and it had leprosy. Leprosy is a skin and nerve disease. Moses put his hand back under his shirt and brought it out healed.

This miracle showed two things. First, the Egyptians saw that Moses had power from God to bring them deadly diseases, but God could also heal them. Second, the Israelites in Egypt were diseased by sin. In God's eyes, this sin was like leprosy. Moses would take them into his heart and they would be cured of sin.

The Lord sent more than just one miracle. This is mercy. God always offers many ways to show people the truth. Jesus did many miracles. So did his early followers. This is because God "wants everyone to be saved and to understand the truth."

Dear God, thank you for your patience with us.

BELONGING TO GOD

Afterward Moses and Aaron went to Pharaoh and said,
"This is what the Lord, the God of Israel, says:
'Let my people go, so that they may hold a festival to me in the desert.'"
EXODUS 5:1 NIV

Remember when Moses was talking with God at the burning bush? He was worried.

"What if the people don't believe that you have sent me?" he asked the Lord. As it turned out, that was no problem. Moses and his brother Aaron were welcomed by Israel. For some reason, Moses didn't worry about what Pharaoh would do when he came. They would soon find out.

They went to Pharaoh, risking their lives. Moses had real reason to be nervous. Forty years before he had murdered an Egyptian. The Pharaoh of that time wanted to kill him for this. Moses ran for his life. Then he came back to demand the freedom of Israel. Would Pharaoh let them go? The people of Israel had been slaves to Pharaoh for a hundred years. He needed them to keep Egypt running. Pharaoh thought they were his people, but he was wrong.

No matter how poor and miserable they were, Israel belonged to God. They were slaves in Egypt, but they didn't belong to Egypt. This is why Moses was there. God would not let his children be trampled on anymore.

Dear God, thank you for rescuing your people.

REMEMBER TO WORSHIP

But the king of Egypt said, "Moses and Aaron,
why are you taking the people away from their labor?
Get back to your work!"
EXODUS 5:4 NIV

Suppose you were the president of a big company. Would you be able to give all your workers a vacation at the same time? Not without some planning. Pharaoh was the same. His country was dependent on its slaves. He couldn't let them go. He was cruel and angry about it, though. He accused the people of being lazy. He said their laziness was why they wanted to worship God. The cities they built for Pharaoh proved they weren't lazy. He only said this so he would have a reason to work them harder. Some people think that others worship God because they have nothing better to do. The truth is that busy people must stop and worship. If they don't, all their work means nothing.

Pharaoh even accused Moses and Aaron of making the people lazy. He told them both, "Get back to work." It didn't matter that they were leaders of Israel. To Pharaoh, they were slaves like all the rest.

Finally, the king made sure the Israelites' lives became even harder. They had to have straw to make bricks. Pharaoh took this away, trying to make them forget about worship. But is it possible for a believer to forget God? No!

Dear God, help me to worship you no matter how busy I am.

CONFUSING TIMES

Moses returned to the LORD and said,
"O Lord, why have you brought trouble upon this people?
Is this why you sent me?
EXODUS 5:22 NIV

Do you think that Moses was confused? He had come to Egypt to free Israel from slavery. Instead of freedom, their lives got much harder. Moses thought about it. "Is this the way God saves Israel? I hoped to be a blessing to them. But I'm a curse. I tried to pull them out of slavery, but I dug the hole deeper."

Moses ran into trouble in Egypt and pulled back. But he didn't retreat any farther than God. He didn't give up, but he argued with God. "Why have you mistreated your own people like this, Lord?" asked Moses. "Why did you send me? I gave Pharaoh your message just as you said. But he's been more brutal to your people than before. You haven't even begun to save them!"

We can learn from this. Sometimes you aren't treated right. When this happens, go to God like Moses did. Talk with God. Here is what God told Moses: "You'll see what I do to Pharaoh. He'll feel my powerful hand upon him. Then he'll let the people go. In fact, he'll want to get rid of them. He'll force them to leave his land!"

Dear God, help me to trust your ways.

GOD WINS

So Moses and Aaron went to see Pharaoh, and they performed the miracle
just as the LORD had told them. Aaron threw down his staff before
Pharaoh and his court, and it became a snake.
Then Pharaoh called in his wise men and magicians,
and they did the same thing with their secret arts.
Their staffs became snakes, too!
But then Aaron's snake swallowed up their snakes.
Pharaoh's heart, however, remained hard and stubborn.
He still refused to listen, just as the LORD had predicted.

EXODUS 7:10–13 NLT

Pharaoh started it all by demanding a miracle. So Aaron threw his walking staff to the ground. Instantly it became a serpent. This should have softened Pharaoh's heart. But right away, Egypt's magicians imitated the miracle, so Pharaoh thought that they were as powerful as Moses. How could this happen?

Remember, God's purpose on earth will move forward when Israel is freed. Yes, the magicians' staffs turned into snakes, but this wasn't a miracle. It was a trick designed to fool Pharaoh and stop God's purpose. The magicians had probably practiced this magic trick for years.

Moses won the contest when the snake, which was Aaron's rod, swallowed the other snakes. Right then, Pharaoh should have taken the side of Moses, but that didn't happen. This miracle still has meaning for us today. The world will play its tricks and people will be fooled. But in the end, God's cause will win!

Dear God, thank you that your cause will win!

THE WATER OF EGYPT

"By this you will know that I am the LORD:
With the staff that is in my hand I will strike the water of the Nile,
and it will be changed into blood."
EXODUS 7:17 NIV

Here is the second miracle that Moses did for Pharaoh. What a terrible thing it is! All the water in Egypt turned to blood. Moses did this right in front of Pharaoh and his servants. Remember, there is nothing secret about our Christian faith. We have no secret codes or handshakes. There are no hush-hush meetings or special teachings. Just like Moses' miracles, everything is out in the open.

Moses simply hit the river with his staff. Amazing! All the waters of Egypt turned to blood—the rivers, canals, ponds, and pools. Even the water in jars and buckets became blood. Again, this miracle has a meaning for Pharaoh and for us. Water is life. Nothing can live without it. Blood that is not inside the body is death. The miracle shows that what is life can turn to death. Water can turn to blood. What is living can die.

Egypt was the most powerful nation in the world. It was alive with religion, culture, and business. A man's walking stick hit the water of the river, and it all died. It turned to blood. And still, Pharaoh was not afraid.

Dear God, help me to respect your awesome power.

LiTTLE THiNGS

"This is what the LORD says: Let my people go, so that they may worship me.
If you refuse to let them go, I will plague your whole country with frogs."

EXODUS 8:1–2 NIV

The great Pharaoh was snowed under with frogs! Such little, ugly things brought mighty Egypt to a stop. God could have plagued Egypt with lions, or bears, or wolves, or with vultures or other huge birds. Instead, frogs covered the land.

The Lord created everything, and he rules it all. The ant God created is as marvelous as the elephant. God's purpose can move forward with the help of a frog or a whale. The power is not in the animal, it is in God.

Why didn't Pharaoh bow down to God when he saw his power taken away by frogs? Since God was his enemy, all God's creatures were at war with him. And the frogs that swarmed over Egypt defeated Pharaoh's mighty army! There were frogs in the palace, in the bedrooms and the beds, in their kitchens and ovens. They were everywhere! This shows that there is nowhere to hide from God. Even under the covers of his bed, Pharaoh found frogs. There is no way he didn't know that God was judging him.

Dear God, thank you for using even the little things to carry out your purpose.

BROKEN PROMISE

But the magicians did the same things by their secret arts;
they also made frogs come up on the land of Egypt.
Pharaoh summoned Moses and Aaron and said,
"Pray to the LORD to take the frogs away from me and my people,
and I will let your people go to offer sacrifices to the LORD."
EXODUS 8:7–8 NIV

Lo and behold! Pharaoh's magicians made frogs come into the land, too. Was this a contest to them? If it was, they weren't opposing Moses; they were opposing God. They could never win that game. Notice that the magicians couldn't make the frogs go away.

Pharaoh asked Moses to pray for him so the frogs would leave. Before, he had said, "Who is the Lord that I should listen to him? I don't know the Lord, and I will not let Israel go." But things changed, and Pharaoh was helpless to get rid of all the frogs. Where else could he turn? He took a step in the right direction and asked Moses to pray to God. And he promised to set Israel free.

Moses and Pharaoh agreed that God would remove the frogs the next day. "Then you will know that no one is as powerful as our God," said Moses. So Moses pleaded with the Lord about the frogs, and the Lord did what Moses asked. The frogs in the houses and the fields all died. There were piles of frogs everywhere and Egypt began to stink like dead frogs. But then Pharaoh saw that the frogs were gone. He thought he didn't need God anymore, and he wouldn't let the people go.

Dear God, help me to keep my promises to you.

TINY BUGS

Aaron stretched out his hand with his rod, and smote the dust of the earth,
and it became lice in man, and in beast; all the dust of the land
became lice throughout all the land of Egypt.
EXODUS 8:17 KJV

This third plague came without warning. Pharaoh had been told about the plagues of blood and of frogs. He had no idea that the dust of his land would suddenly turn to lice. Aaron took his rod and hit the dust with it. All the dust became lice! The people of Egypt and the animals were covered with lice.

Lice are tiny bugs that you can hardly see. They cause awful itching. Sometimes a school will become infested with head lice. The students all must be checked for lice. If they have lice, they must go home until the lice are gone. Special shampoos are supposed to kill them, but these don't work very well. The only sure way to get rid of head lice is to check every hair. If there are lice on a hair, they must be removed, one by one.

The magicians were helpless. "This is the finger of God!" they cried to Pharaoh. It was not the strong arm of God, or even God's hand. This plague was so very terrible, but it was only the little finger of God! Pharaoh didn't change. His heart was still hard and stubborn. He wouldn't listen.

Dear God, help me to always listen to you.

FLIES!

"Let my people go, so they can worship me. If you refuse,
I will send swarms of flies throughout Egypt.
Your homes will be filled with them,
and the ground will be covered with them."

EXODUS 8:20–21 NLT

Pharaoh simply would not do what God asked.

Early in the morning, Moses went to the river and spoke with Pharaoh. This shows again that God doesn't work in secret. Moses was face-to-face with the king of Egypt, outdoors for all to see. This time, God made a difference between the Egyptians and the Hebrews. The flies would not go into the Israelites' land. Flies are impossible to control. They go where they want and can't be moved elsewhere. But nothing is impossible for God. He controlled billions of flies, and they did not bother the Hebrews.

God's enemy, Satan, has another name—Beelzebub. This name means, "The lord of the flies." But the lord of the flies could do nothing for Pharaoh. Terrible swarms of flies flew into Pharaoh's palace and into every home in Egypt. The flies ruined the whole country. All these plagues are pictures of the way God will judge the earth. The Bible describes how he will call for the flies that are down the river in Egypt. And bees will come from the land of Assyria.

Dear God, thank you for controlling every little thing—even flies!

THE ANIMALS' PLAGUE

*"If you refuse to let them go and continue to hold them back,
the hand of the LORD will bring a terrible plague on your livestock in the field—
on your horses and donkeys and camels and on your cattle and sheep and goats."*
EXODUS 9:2–3 NIV

The blood, frogs, lice, and flies were awful. But it didn't matter. Pharaoh still wouldn't let the people go free. Soon, the other plagues would seem like nothing at all. The next day, every one of the Egyptian's animals died.

Pharaoh was stubborn and the Egyptians sinned. But what did the gentle sheep do to deserve death? The truth is that all the creation was dragged down when humanity sinned. A man once sang, "How long will the land weep? Even the grass in the field is dead. The people who live in this land are wicked. The animals and birds are swept away because of it." This is a great tragedy.

All the animals died in Egypt. Suddenly the Egyptians were as poor as the Hebrews. Their animals were like money to them, so when they were gone, the Egyptians had nothing. Even their land was no good to them because the farm animals were all dead. The farmers couldn't plow or harvest. Soon, Egypt would have no food.

The Egyptians worshiped animals such as dogs, cats, and cattle. So this plague that killed the Egyptians' animals killed the Egyptian worship, too. Israel couldn't worship and neither could Egypt.

Dear God, thank you that I have the freedom to worship you.

THE BiG OUCH

*Then the Lord said to Moses and Aaron, "Take handfuls of soot
from a furnace and have Moses toss it into the air in the presence of Pharaoh.
It will become fine dust over the whole land of Egypt,
and festering boils will break out on men and animals throughout the land."*

EXODUS 9:8–9 NIV

These stories in Exodus show how strong the world's system is. Egypt is like the world around us. Look how strong she was when

all these plagues came. One after another they came—blood instead of water, frogs stinking up the land, lice and flies swarming everywhere, and dead animals. Still, Pharaoh was strong and stubborn. He wouldn't let the people go out to worship God.

The suffering was not over for Egypt. A few handfuls of ashes were tossed in the air. Then, out of the air, like out of nowhere, came a disease on the Egyptians' skin.

Painful blisters were on everyone. These were so awful that they would always be called the boils of Egypt. The Bible mentions that the magicians were covered with the boils. The magicians had played a game with Moses. "We are better magicians than you are," they seemed to say. But with the boils on their skin, they must have known they were playing with God.

Still, Pharaoh wouldn't let Israel go to worship the Lord.

Dear God, thank you that you are stronger than anyone or anything in this world.

HAIL TO THE CHIEF

*"You still set yourself against my people and will not let them go.
Therefore, at this time tomorrow I will send the worst hailstorm
that has ever fallen on Egypt."*
EXODUS 9:17–18 NIV

Pharaoh thought he could keep the Hebrews in slavery. He took away the straw and forced them to make more bricks than ever. But then there was no need for bricks in Egypt. The land was nearly ruined.

More plagues were on the way. Maybe the worst plague of all came to Pharaoh alone. It wasn't a disease on his body. It was worse than losing all his cattle. It was a deep damage to his soul. God hardened his heart. It had no feeling; it had no hope.

Pharaoh was a great king who was worshiped as a god, while God's people were poor slaves. Look at what happened when Pharaoh turned against Israel. His nation was ruined and his heart was ruined, too. Opposing Israel was the same as opposing God.

Yet another plague came. Hail fell and lightning flashed. It was the worst storm Egypt had ever seen. Hail struck both men and animals. It beat down everything growing in the fields and stripped every tree. The only place it didn't hail was Goshen, where the Israelites lived.

Dear God, thank you for protecting your people.

GOOD HEART, BAD HEART

Then Pharaoh urgently sent for Moses and Aaron. "I finally admit my fault,"
he confessed. "The LORD is right, and my people and I are wrong.
Please beg the LORD to end this terrifying thunder and hail.
I will let you go at once."
EXODUS 9:27–28 NLT

Here were two men, Pharaoh and Moses, and a disaster. Look at how these two treated each other in this crisis. "I finally admit I'm wrong," Pharaoh told the man of God. "The Lord is right, and I am wrong. Moses, please beg God to end this awful thunder and hail. I'll let Israel go free right away."

This sounded good. It seemed Pharaoh had finally seen the light.

"All right," Moses replied. "When I leave the city, I'll lift my hands and pray. Then the thunder and hail will stop. This will prove to you that God controls the earth. But I want you to know that I know you still don't fear the Lord." So, Moses left the city and lifted his hands to pray. Right then, the thunder and hail stopped.

Moses was honest. He did what he said he would do. He had a good heart.

When Pharaoh saw the hail had stopped, he sinned again. He stubbornly refused to do what he promised and let the people leave. Pharaoh lied because his heart was hard toward God.

Dear God, help me to be honest.

iGNORiNG ADViCE

*The court officials now came to Pharaoh and appealed to him.
"How long will you let these disasters go on?
Please let the Israelites go to serve the LORD their God!
Don't you realize that Egypt lies in ruins?"*

EXODUS 10:7 NLT

Pharaoh's assistants finally tried to talk with Pharaoh. God had hardened their king's heart, but they didn't know it. They may have thought Pharaoh was crazy. Otherwise, why would he let his country be ruined by the plagues? The assistants knew that Moses was nothing but trouble, even if Pharaoh didn't know it. They said to him, "Don't you know that Egypt has been destroyed?" Israel was like a heavy stone. These men had stood by and watched as Pharaoh tried to lift it. Their king had hurt himself under its weight.

So sad, hard-hearted Pharaoh tried again to make a deal with Moses. He said, "Okay, you can go and worship your God. But only the men can go. Women and children must stay in Egypt. Your animals have to stay, too." He wanted to be sure that the men would come back. Their families would be his hostages.

Moses disagreed. "We are going to have a feast, and our families must feast with us. And what are we going eat if we don't have our animals?"

There was no way that Pharaoh would allow every single Israelite to leave. So he ignored his own assistant's advice and his doom was sealed.

Dear God, help me to listen to good advice.

LOCUST INVASION

*And the Lord said to Moses, "Stretch out your hand over Egypt
so that locusts will swarm over the land and devour everything
growing in the fields, everything left by the hail."*

EXODUS 10:12–13 NIV

My great-grandfather Samuel was a farmer in Washington, Kansas. A plague of locusts came when he first moved there from Pennsylvania in the early 1870s. Locusts are flying grasshoppers. During that awful plague, the locusts swarmed so thickly that they blocked out the sun. They ate the wood from my grandfather's barn and the clothes off his body. They devoured all the plant life. This was horrific. My great-grandmother, Eliza, took her children and fled back to Pennsylvania. She returned when the plague was over.

Locust plagues still happen today. The country of Australia just had a plague in the year 2000. That country tries to control locusts by spraying the locusts with chemicals to kill them before they can fly.

In Egypt, there had already been a hailstorm like no other before it. In a hailstorm, balls of ice fall from the sky. These can be as small as a pea or as big as a baseball. Hail strips the leaves from trees and crushes the plants on the ground. Do you think there was any food left in Egypt for the locusts? What little was left, the locusts ate. Egypt was stripped bare of all plant life. God is just and fair. He was seriously punishing Egypt for not letting his people go.

Dear God, thank you for being just and fair.

LEADER OF A NATION

Then the LORD said to Moses,
"Stretch out your hand toward the sky
so that darkness will spread over Egypt—
darkness that can be felt."
EXODUS 10:21 NIV

In many ways, Egypt was a country like any other. People lived there on farms, in cities, and in towns. They had families and homes like anyone else. What happened to them was a great tragedy. People lost everything they had because Pharaoh had hardened his heart toward God. This brought darkness upon the country.

The Egyptians had no choice about who the pharaoh would be. Not only so, he was more than just a king. Everyone thought that Pharaoh was a god and so they worshiped him. Today, the leaders of nations don't say that they are gods. Still, their hearts can be hardened toward God. Many of them don't even care what the people of their country want. They do and say whatever they please.

Here in the United States, we can choose our leaders. A certain day comes every four years when we have elections. On that day, we vote for the men and women who wish to lead us. The story of Egypt teaches that a leader can change everything for an entire country. So be sure your parents vote on Election Day. When you turn eighteen years old, you be sure to vote, too.

Dear God, thank you for the freedom to choose the leaders of our country.

A LAMB THAT SAVES

"Each family must choose a lamb or a young goat for a sacrifice.
Then each family in the community must slaughter its lamb."
EXODUS 12:3, 6 NLT

Pharaoh was so stubborn, nothing that God did had budged him. The Lord had sent disaster after disaster upon that country. Still, Pharaoh would not let the people go. Still, the Israelites were slaves.

What could save the people of Israel from Egypt?

A little lamb was the secret. Moses told Pharaoh, "Here's what the Lord says to you: About midnight I will pass through Egypt. Every firstborn son will die in every family in Egypt, from the oldest son of Pharaoh, who sits on the throne, to the oldest son of his lowliest slave. Even the firstborn of the animals will die." The firstborn son is the oldest child in a family.

Then God told Pharaoh, "A loud wail will be heard all over Egypt. There has never been such a sound before, and there never will be again."

What would save the Israelites from this disaster? A lamb for every Jewish family. Though this sounds awful, every family was to kill their lamb and then paint a little of the lamb's blood on their doors. God saw the blood on the doors and those houses were saved from death. So a lamb saved Israel, just like the Lamb of God, Jesus, would later save the world.

Dear God, thank you for saving your people with a precious Lamb.

UNDERSTANDING JESUS

*"Then they are to take some of the blood and put it on the sides
and tops of the doorframes of the houses where they eat the lambs."*
EXODUS 12:7 NIV

Lambs died in Egypt so the people of Israel could live. Their death made two things happen: First, the Israelites put the lambs' blood on their doors. This caused death to pass over their houses. Second, they ate the roasted meat of the lambs. This gave them strength to follow God and leave Egypt.

Thousands of years ago, far away in Egypt, this happened to Israel. So why is it important to us today? Here's why: The same things happen when a person believes in Jesus. The story of Israel in Egypt helps us to understand our own experience. God loved us so much that he gave us Jesus, the Lamb of God. Jesus died so that everyone who believes in him can have eternal life. Believing in him is like putting the lamb's blood on the door. Death passes us by. Jesus is also like food. Anyone who believes in him is strengthened to follow God in this world.

The Bible is full of stories about the children of Israel. These are not just stories, though. They are told so that we will have examples to live by. When we read stories about Israel we can understand more about Christ.

Dear God, thank you for the Bible, which helps me learn about you.

SO OTHERS CAN LIVE

*"When the LORD goes through the land to strike down the Egyptians,
he will see the blood on the top and sides of the doorframe
and will pass over that doorway, and he will not permit
the destroyer to enter your houses and strike you down."*

EXODUS 12:23 NIV

When you sit down to eat supper with your family, do you enjoy the food? Are you thankful for the food that keeps you alive? I hope so. Do you know that things must die so you can have food? Plants and animals die to make food so that you can live. This is the truth—death brings life.

Remember Genesis chapter three? There, Adam and Eve disobeyed God—they had sinned, and they were naked. God then killed animals and covered the man and woman with these animals' skins. The animals that died may have been lambs, whose soft skins make good clothing. Their death is called a *sacrifice*. Because of this, Adam and Eve could live.

The Bible tells about many sacrifices. The first was in the Garden of Eden with Adam and Eve. In the book of Exodus, another important sacrifice occurs. Here, lambs are killed so the people of Israel will not die with the Egyptians. Both of these sacrifices happened so that people could live. And they both point forward in time to the sacrifice of another Lamb. This one is called the Lamb of God. He is Jesus Christ who, like the lambs in Egypt, died so we can live.

Dear God, thank you that Jesus died so that I can live.

SPECIAL PEOPLE

Pharaoh and all his officials and all the Egyptians got up during the night,
and there was loud wailing in Egypt,
for there was not a house without someone dead.

EXODUS 12:30 NIV

Nine plagues had come upon Pharaoh and his nation—blood, frogs, lice, flies, disease, boils, thunderous hail, locusts, and darkness. Egypt was nearly destroyed by these. What a hard heart Pharaoh must have had! He would not let Israel go, no matter what. That is, until the tenth plague came.

At midnight, God passed through Egypt. All the oldest sons died in every family in the land. The oldest son of Pharaoh, who was the king on the throne, died. The oldest son of his lowest slave died, too. This was the tenth plague. People cried aloud all over Egypt. The Bible says there had never been such crying before and there never will be again. But in the houses of the Israelites, it was peaceful. Not even a dog barked. This shows there was a difference between the Egyptians and the Israelites.

Many hundreds of years before, God called Abraham from a place known as Ur in Chaldea. Abraham followed God to a new land called Canaan. There, God promised Abraham that he would have a huge family. From this family Jesus Christ would be born. This is why Israel is different from Egypt or any other nation.

Dear God, thank you for making your people special.

A DAY TO CELEBRATE

That night the people of Israel left Rameses and started for Succoth.
There were about 600,000 men, plus all the women and children.
And they were all traveling on foot.
EXODUS 12:37 NLT

Nearly one and a half million people followed Moses out of Egypt. They had no time to pack or prepare. When they ate the lamb that night, they were in a hurry. Even their bread had no time to rise. They took the raw dough with them. When it was finally baked, it came out more like crackers than bread.

Imagine all those people hurrying along in the middle of the night. They carried all they had in their hands or on their backs. No one had prepared any food to take along. With them were herds of animals—goats and sheep and cattle—millions of animals! Choking dust rose all around. It was noisy. Children were crying, animals were braying, men were shouting, and women called out. None of them really knew where they were going.

The Israelites had lived in Egypt for 430 years. Suddenly they went out of that land. The Bible says, "This night had been reserved by the Lord to bring his people out from the land of Egypt." It was as if God had been waiting all those years, waiting for this very day to come. Ever since then, the Jews have celebrated this day. It is called Passover.

Dear God, thank you for the Passover.

DEDICATED TO THE LORD

"In days to come, when your son asks you, 'What does this mean?' say to him,
'With a mighty hand the LORD brought us out of Egypt,
out of the land of slavery."
EXODUS 13:14 NIV

God wanted the people never to forget this day. It was the day death passed over their houses. They didn't die because of the lambs' blood on their doorways. But the oldest child in every Egyptian family did die. So Moses told the Israelites, "That is why we now offer all the firstborn males to the LORD—except that the firstborn sons are always redeemed." This means that the newborn children were all dedicated to God. Jews have been doing this ever since the first Passover.

We also dedicate ourselves to the Lord. We do it for the same reason the Jews did that day. We give ourselves to God because he saved us. Jesus Christ is like the lambs that died on that first Passover. He died for us so that we will not have to die. This was just like the way God saved Israel from Egypt. Death has passed us by and we belong to God forever.

Dear God, thank you that I belong to you.

WATER FROM A ROCK

The LORD guided them by a pillar of cloud during the day
and a pillar of fire at night.

EXODUS 13:21 NLT

When the children of Israel escaped Egypt, they knew exactly which way to go. The Lord guided them day and night. During the day, they followed a pillar of cloud. At night, it became a pillar of fire. This pillar may have looked like a huge pine tree that was made out of cloud and fire.

Even though they knew God was leading them, the Israelites were often afraid and tired of their journey. Once they came to a place called Rephidim. There was no water there, so they complained to Moses, "Give us water to drink!" They were sorry they'd ever left Egypt and thought that they would die.

Moses didn't know what to do. "What should I do with these people?" he cried to God. "They are about to stone me!"

"Take your shepherd's staff and walk ahead of the people," the Lord answered. "I'll meet you by the rock at Mount Sinai. Strike the rock, and water will come pouring out." Sure enough, water gushed out of the rock.

Today, Jesus Christ is like that rock. He provides the water that we need to never be thirsty again. He said, "But the water I give them takes away thirst altogether. It becomes a perpetual spring within them, giving them eternal life."

Dear God, thank you for your son, Jesus, who gives us eternal life.

GOD IS ALL YOU NEED

The LORD hardened the heart of Pharaoh king of Egypt,
so that he pursued the Israelites, who were marching out boldly.

EXODUS 14:8 NIV

Pharaoh saw that the Israelites were really leaving. So he took six hundred of Egypt's best chariots with him, and he chased after the people of Israel. All of Pharaoh's army—his horses, chariots, and charioteers—were in the chase. They caught up with the people of Israel as they were camped beside the seashore.

Pharaoh and his army approached. The people could see them in the distance, marching toward them. They panicked and cried to the Lord for help.

Then they turned against Moses. "Why did you bring us out here to die in the wilderness?" they complained. "Why did you make us leave? Didn't we tell you to leave us alone while we were in Egypt? Slavery was better than dying out here in the wilderness!"

But Moses told them, "Don't be afraid. Just stand where you are and watch the Lord rescue you. You see the Egyptians today. But they'll never be seen again. The Lord will fight for you. You won't even have to lift a finger!"

The Israelites had left Egypt with nothing. They didn't even have any food. But they had God. In the end, that is really all you need.

Dear God, thank you for being everything that I need.

WALLS OF WATER

Then the LORD said to Moses, "Why are you crying out to me?
Tell the Israelites to move on. Raise your staff and stretch out your hand
over the sea to divide the water so that the Israelites can go
through the sea on dry ground."
EXODUS 14:15–16 NIV

The book of Exodus is named for the most exciting story in the Bible. The word *exodus* means "a journey by a large group to escape from a harsh situation." The Israelites' escape from Egypt is called the Exodus.

All those people followed an angel of God with a pillar of cloud

during the day. At night, it was a pillar of fire. The Lord made sure they all could see it.

Pharaoh's army was menacing Israel. So the angel of God moved behind Israel. The pillar of cloud also moved around behind them. The cloud settled between the Israelite and Egyptian camps.

Night came. The pillar of cloud turned into a pillar of fire so the Israelites had light. But the cloud brought darkness to the Egyptians. They couldn't find the Israelites. Then Moses raised his hand over the sea. God opened a path through the water with a strong wind. The wind blew all night. The seabed turned into dry land. So the people of Israel walked through the sea on dry ground through walls of water on each side!

Dear God, thank you for your awesome miracles!

INTO THE SEA

*The Egyptians pursued them, and all Pharaoh's horses
and chariots and horsemen followed them into the sea.*
EXODUS 14:23 NIV

Why didn't Pharaoh and his army give up the chase? The sea had turned to dry land! Here's why: God said, "I will harden the hearts of the Egyptians, and they will follow the Israelites into the sea. Then I will receive great glory."

So all of Pharaoh's horses, chariots, and charioteers followed them. The whole army charged across the bottom of the sea. Early in the morning, the Lord looked down from the pillar of fire and cloud. Then God threw the Egyptians into chaos. Their chariot wheels began to come off, and the chariots were impossible to drive. "Let's get out of here!" the Egyptians shouted. "The Lord is fighting for Israel!"

All the Israelites got safely to the other side of the sea. The Lord said to Moses, "Raise your hand over the sea again. Then it will rush back over the Egyptians and their chariots."

The sun was rising when Moses raised his hand over the sea. The waters roared back into their place, and the Lord swept the terrified Egyptians into the surging sea. The waters covered the entire army of Pharaoh. Not one Egyptian who had chased the Israelites into the sea survived.

Dear God, thank you for defeating your enemies.

SONG OF VICTORY

And when the Israelites saw the great power the LORD
displayed against the Egyptians, the people feared the LORD
and put their trust in him and in Moses his servant.
EXODUS 14:31 NIV

Everybody was safe on the other side of the sea. They were free
from slavery in Egypt! Then Moses and the people of Israel sang
this song to the Lord:

"I will sing to the LORD, for he has triumphed gloriously;
    he has thrown both horse and rider into the sea.
The LORD is my strength and my song;
    he has become my victory.
He is my God, and I will praise him;
    he is my father's God, and I will exalt him!
The LORD is a warrior;
    yes, the LORD is his name!"

"Who else among the gods is like you, O LORD?
    Who is glorious in holiness like you—
so awesome in splendor,
    performing such wonders?
You raised up your hand,
    and the earth swallowed our enemies.
With unfailing love you will lead
    this people whom you have ransomed.
You will guide them in your strength
    to the place where your holiness dwells."

Dear God, thank you for rescuing your people from Egypt.

TAKING OUR PUNISHMENT

So Moses returned to the LORD and said,
"Alas, these people have committed a terrible sin.
They have made gods of gold for themselves.
But now, please forgive their sin—and if not,
then blot me out of the record you are keeping."

EXODUS 32:31–32 NLT

When my son was about ten years old, he decided to lead his friends in smashing jack-o'-lanterns at Halloween. He did the wrong thing. But when he was caught, I was at the police station right away. I wanted to be sure he was treated fairly.

Moses did this when Israel worshiped the golden calf. Moses was even willing to take their punishment. I've sometimes wished that I could take my children's place because I didn't want them to suffer. But this was not possible for me. Not even Moses could do it. Only Jesus could do this.

In his death on the cross, Jesus did what no one had ever done before. Never again will anyone do this. He took our place in God's judgment. He did this for all people. The Bible says, "God made Christ, who never sinned, to be the offering for our sin, so that we could be made right with God."

We cannot take the place of the people we love. Their troubles are their own. But we can pray for them because of Jesus' love.

Dear God, thank you for Jesus, who took my punishment.

DAILY PRAYERS

Whenever the ark set out, Moses said, "Rise up, O LORD! . . .
Whenever it came to rest, he said, "Return, O LORD."
NUMBERS 10:35–36 NIV

Every day is a journey. It begins in the morning the moment your feet touch the floor at your bedside. When you lift them into bed again that night, the journey is over. Most days, our journeys are just about the same as the day before. This is not like the journey of the people of Israel. Then, Moses prayed for the people at the beginning and the end of each day so that all of Israel's journeys were covered with prayer. Ours should be, too.

Moses' prayers were very simple. Ours don't need to be fancy, either. "Rise up, Lord," Moses prayed in the morning, "Let your enemies be scattered." Our morning prayer can be like this, too. Let's ask Jesus Christ to protect us. He died, came back from death, and is now in heaven with the Father. He did this so he could protect us each day.

When evening came, Moses prayed, "Return, O Lord." This can be our nightly prayer, too. Someday, Jesus will return to this world. We can pray for Jesus' wonderful return each night before bed.

Dear God, please protect us on our journeys and come back for us soon.

THE PROMISED LAND

The LORD said to Moses, "Send some men to explore the land of Canaan,
which I am giving to the Israelites.
From each ancestral tribe send one of its leaders."
NUMBERS 13:1–2 NIV

In the Exodus, the Israelites were freed from slavery in Egypt. But this was not the only reason they escaped. God wanted them to go to the Promised Land—the country called Canaan. God promised this country to Abraham and his children. Since the Israelites are the family of Abraham, this was their land.

The Israelites traveled to a place that was near Canaan. From there, Moses sent some men to explore the land. "Go north into the hill country. See what the land is like," he told them. "Find out whether the people living there are strong or weak. How many are there? What kind of land is it? Do their towns have walls or not? Are there many trees? Be bold, and bring back samples of the crops you see."

So they went to spy out the land. When they came to the valley of Eshcol, they cut down a cluster of grapes. It was so huge that it took two of them to carry it! They also took samples of pomegranates and figs. The Israelites renamed that valley "Cluster" because of the cluster of grapes these men cut there.

The Promised Land was a wonderful place!

Dear God, thank you for the Promised Land.

FEELING AFRAID

This was their report to Moses:
"We arrived in the land you sent us to see,
and it is indeed a magnificent country—
a land flowing with milk and honey."
NUMBERS 13:27 NLT

The Bible is not like any other book. It isn't a fairy tale or a fable. Its stories don't always have a happy ending. Yes, the Promised Land was a rich country. It was as if milk and honey flowed there. But that wasn't the whole story.

After exploring the Promised Land for forty days, the men returned. They showed everyone what they'd seen. The whole nation saw the fruit they had taken from the land. "But the people living there are powerful," they said. "Their cities and towns are large forts."

Caleb, the leader of the spies, encouraged the people. "Let's go right away and take this land," he said. "We can take it!"

But the other men who had explored the land didn't want to do this. "We can't go against them!" they said. "They are stronger than we are!" So they made the Israelites feel bad about the land. "The land we saw will swallow us up. All the people we saw were huge. We even saw giants! We felt like grasshoppers next to them, and that's what we looked like to them!"

All the people began weeping, and they cried all night. They were afraid and would not go into the Promised Land.

Dear God, help me not to be afraid of what you want me to do.

KEPT FROM CANAAN

"We wish we had died in Egypt, or even here in the wilderness!" they wailed.
"Why is the LORD taking us to this country only to have us die in battle?
Our wives and little ones will be carried off as slaves!
Let's get out of here and return to Egypt!"
NUMBERS 14:2–3 NLT

The worst thing that *could* happen *did* happen. Israel refused to do what God wanted. They wouldn't go into the Promised Land.

Moses fell face down on the ground in front of everybody. Joshua and Caleb tore their clothes. "If the Lord is happy with us, he'll bring us into that land safely," they called out. "It is a rich land flowing with milk and honey. He'll give it to us! Don't go against God, and don't be afraid of the people in the land. They are helpless! They have no protection. But the Lord is with us! Don't be afraid of them!"

But everybody talked about killing Joshua and Caleb. Then God appeared to all the Israelites! "How long will these people turn away from me?" God asked Moses. "Will they never believe me, even after all the miracles I've done for them? I will wash my hands of them and destroy them with a plague."

God didn't kill the children of Israel. But he didn't let them go into the good land of Canaan, either. They left that place and wandered in the wilderness for forty years. By then, the people who'd been afraid to go into the land had died.

Dear God, help me to always believe you.

A NEW GENERATION

The LORD said to Joshua. . ."Moses my servant is dead.
Now then, you and all these people, get ready to cross the Jordan River
into the land I am about to give to them—to the Israelites."

JOSHUA 1:1–2 NIV

Finally, the children of Israel entered the Promised Land. Hundreds of years had passed since God promised the land to Abraham. Now, his family was going to own it.

The people set out to cross the Jordan River. These people were much different than the ones who had escaped from Egypt. Forty years before, the people of the Exodus refused to go into the land. So they wandered in the wilderness, grew old, and died. Their children grew up to be the ones to take the land.

Plus, the Israelites had learned to worship God. They had God's Law and a special tent where they could worship. They also had a wooden box covered and decorated with gold, which was called the Ark of the Covenant. God's Law was kept in it.

So they went into the Promised Land. Priests with the Ark led them across the Jordan River. When their feet touched the rushing water, the water stopped flowing! It collected upstream. Downriver, the riverbed was dry. All the people crossed over the river near the city of Jericho. Meanwhile, the priests who carried the Ark stood on dry ground in the middle of the riverbed. They waited there until everyone had crossed the Jordan on dry ground.

Dear God, thank you for giving us second chances.

STONES FOR REMEMBERING

The LORD had said to Joshua, "Command the priests carrying the Ark of the Covenant to come up out of the riverbed." So Joshua gave the command. And as soon as the priests carrying the Ark of the LORD's covenant came up out of the riverbed, the Jordan River flooded its banks as before.

JOSHUA 4:15–18 NLT

The people of Israel crossed the Jordan River on the tenth day of the first month. This was the same month of the Exodus from Egypt. They all camped at a place called Gilgal, which was east of Jericho.

Before the priests came out of the riverbed, men hauled out twelve huge stones. There at Gilgal, Joshua piled up these stones. Then he said to the Israelites, "In the future, your children will wonder, 'What do these stones mean?' You can tell them this: 'This is where the Israelites crossed the Jordan on dry ground. The Lord dried up the river right before their eyes. He kept it dry until all were across. This is just like the time of the Exodus. Then, he dried up the Red Sea until we had all crossed over. God did this so that all the nations on earth can know the power of the Lord. This happened so that you will be in awe of the Lord forever.' "

Israel began to live in the land called Canaan. They built homes and towns and farmed the land for hundreds of years to come.

Dear God, help us to remember all that you have done for us.

SONGS OF PRAISE

On that day Deborah and Barak son of Abinoam sang this song:
"When the princes in Israel take the lead,
when the people willingly offer themselves—praise the LORD!
Hear this, you kings! Listen, you rulers!
I will sing to the LORD, I will sing;
I will make music to the LORD, the God of Israel."

JUDGES 5:1–3 NIV

When my little boy was born, he lay in my arms wrapped in a blanket. I was sitting in a rocking chair by the side of his mother's bed. The three of us were alone there. We had been in the hospital seventeen minutes. Imagine how quickly he was born!

I began to sing hymns of love. I gave thanks. I praised God. My prayers were no bigger than my baby, and they were soft like his blanket. There was nothing else I could do but praise God!

When Deborah sang her song, it was the same. She had won a great victory over Israel's enemies. The war was done. All was well. At a time like that, praise is easy. It is an honest response to God's work.

The Song of Deborah is one of the oldest writings in the Bible. It was written when the Israelites defeated the Caananites at Taanach. For twenty years, the Caananites had controlled Israel. The people suffered. No one had courage enough to stand with God against this enemy. The people were silent and unbelieving. Then Deborah rose up and defeated the Caananites. Then the land was at peace for forty years.

Dear God, I sing praises to you!

THE JUDGES

"This is what the LORD, the God of Israel, says: I brought you up out of Egypt,
out of the land of slavery. I said to you, 'I am the LORD your God;
do not worship the gods of the Amorites, in whose land you live.'
But you have not listened to me."

JUDGES 6:8, 10 NIV

All through the Bible, God gives reminders of what he has done for us.

You remember the story of Israel in Egypt. They were slaves there, making bricks and building cities. Their suffering was terrible. God knew they were suffering and sent Moses to rescue them. Moses showed Pharaoh miracles and signs, but Pharaoh would not let the children of Israel go.

Finally came the day of the Passover. The Israelite families all killed a lamb. They put the blood of those lambs on the doorways of their houses. But the Egyptians had no lamb's blood on their doors. God passed over Egypt and death came to every house that had no lamb. This is how God brought Israel out of slavery in Egypt.

The book of Judges tells that Israel forgot what God did for them. This happened again and again, and Israel suffered because of their forgetfulness. But God did not forget Israel. People like Deborah, Gideon, and Samson brought Israel back to God. These people were called judges.

Today, it is still easy to forget what God has done. We don't have judges, though. We have the Bible to remind us every day what God has done.

Dear God, help me to read my Bible every day and never forget about you.

GIVING GOD ALL

The angel of the LORD came and sat down under the oak in Ophrah. . .
where. . .Gideon was threshing wheat in a winepress to keep it from
the Midianites. When the angel of the Lord appeared to Gideon,
he said, "The Lord is with you, mighty warrior."

JUDGES 6:11–12 NIV

One day, the angel of the Lord sat under an oak tree in Ophrah. Gideon was nearby in the bottom of a winepress. A winepress was a large, smooth, shallow pit in the ground. He was trying to hide his grain from the Midianites, who were enemies of Israel.

The angel said, "Mighty hero, the Lord is with you!"

"Sir," Gideon replied, "if the Lord is with us, why are we suffering? Where are all the miracles our ancestors told us about? The Midianites rule us now."

The Lord said, "You go and rescue Israel from the Midianites. I'm sending you!"

"But Lord," Gideon replied, "How can I? My clan is the weakest of all. I'm the least in my whole family!"

"I'll be with you," The Lord answered. "You will destroy the Midianites as if you were fighting against one man."

Gideon replied, "Don't go away. I'm going to get an offering for you." The Lord promised, "I'll stay right here."

Gideon didn't have much to offer to the Lord. He was the lowest man in a weak clan. He was hiding from the Midianites in a winepress, a hole in the ground. But he offered himself to God. For God, this was enough.

Dear God, I may not have much, but I want to offer all of me to you.

TRUST GOD'S PROMISES

Gideon said to God, "If you will save Israel by my hand as you have promised—
look, I will place a wool fleece on the threshing floor.
If there is dew only on the fleece and all the ground is dry,
then I will know that you will save Israel by my hand,
as you said." And that is what happened.

JUDGES 6:36–38 NIV

Soon, the armies of Midian crossed the Jordan to attack Israel. They camped in the Jezreel Valley. Then the Lord's Spirit took over Gideon. He blew a ram's horn as a call to war. Men from his clan came to him. Gideon then sent messengers to call for warriors from other tribes. All of them came to fight Midian.

Even though all these soldiers came to fight, Gideon's faith was suddenly weak. A strong army wasn't enough for him. Gideon had to be sure God was with him in the fight.

This reminds me of a famous Bible verse, "'Not by might nor by power, but by my Spirit,' says the LORD Almighty." Somehow, Gideon knew that the entire world's might and power was not enough. He wasn't afraid to say he needed more faith in God.

You can tell God the same thing. God wants you to be sure that he will never change his mind. So God gave you both his promise and his oath written in the Bible. Gideon didn't have the Bible, so he put out a fleece. But you can trust God's promises in the Bible.

Dear God, thank you for proving that you are God.

GOD'S WAYS—NOT OURS

The LORD said to Gideon, "You have too many warriors with you.
If I let all of you fight the Midianites, the Israelites will boast to me
that they saved themselves by their own strength."
JUDGES 7:2 NLT

Gideon had thirty-two thousand soldiers in his army. This number was much less than the army of Midian. But this battle was not going to be fought by Israel's army. The battle would teach Israel to trust God again. They would learn, "'Not by might nor by power, but by my Spirit,' says the LORD Almighty."

Even after twenty-two thousand men left, God said Gideon had too many soldiers. "Bring them to the spring," said God. "I'll decide who'll go with you."

Gideon took his warriors down to the water. There, the Lord told him, "Divide them into two groups. In one, put those who cup water in their hands to drink. In the other, put those who kneel and drink with their mouths in the stream." Only three hundred of the men drank from their hands. The others got on their knees and drank with their mouths in the stream.

The Lord told Gideon, "I'll give you victory over the Midianites with these three hundred men. Send all the others home." This shows that God's ways are much different than ours. So, Gideon collected the ram's horns of the other warriors and sent them home. But he kept the three hundred men with him.

Dear God, help us to trust you even though your ways are not our ways.

A LITTLE LOAF

His friend said, "Your dream can mean only one thing—
God has given Gideon. . .victory over all the armies united with Midian!"
When Gideon heard the dream and its interpretation, he thanked God.

JUDGES 7:14–15 NLT

The Midianite camp was in the valley just below the Israelites. During the night, the Lord told Gideon, "Get up! Go down into the Midianite camp. I've given you victory over them! If you're afraid to attack, go to their camp. Listen to what they're saying and you'll be sure you can win."

So Gideon went down to the edge of the enemy camp. The armies there were like a swarm of locusts. Their camels were like grains of sand on the beach—too many to count! Gideon snuck up just as a man was telling his friend about a dream.

"I had this dream," the man said. "A loaf of barley bread came tumbling down into our camp. It hit a tent and knocked it flat!"

His friend said, "Your dream can mean only one thing. God has given Gideon victory over the army of Midian!"

Gideon heard this and thanked God. Then he returned to the Israelite camp. "Get up!" he shouted, "The Lord has given you victory over the Midianites!"

Just as when he was hiding in the winepress, Gideon didn't have much. In the dream, his army was like a little loaf of bread. But this was enough for God to bring victory.

Dear God, thank you that you can use anything to bring victory for you and your people.

THE SWORD OF THE LORD

When I blow with a trumpet, I and all that are with me,
then blow ye the trumpets also on every side of all the camp, and say,
The sword of the LORD, and of Gideon.

JUDGES 7:18 KJV

It was midnight. The guard in the Midianite camp had just changed. Gideon and the men with him reached the edge of the Midianite camp. Suddenly, they blew their horns and broke their clay jars. Then the rest of the Israelites blew their horns and broke their jars. They held their blazing torches in their left hands and their ram's horns in their right hands. "A sword for the Lord and for Gideon!" they shouted.

Each man stood around the camp and watched. The Midianites

rushed around in a panic, shouting as they ran. The three hundred Israelites blew their horns. The warriors in the camp fought with their swords. Those who weren't killed ran as far as they could. Then Gideon sent for the warriors who had been sent away. These joined in chasing after the fleeing army of Midian.

Their battle cry was, "A sword for the Lord and for Gideon!" Notice that there is only one sword. It is a sword for the Lord and it is for Gideon, too. The Lord fought the battle, but he used Gideon to do this. Together they used one sword. For us today, this one sword is the Word of God.

Dear God, thank you for the sword of the Spirit, which is your Word.

YOU CAN'T SAVE YOURSELF

But Gideon told them, "I will not rule over you,
nor will my son rule over you.
The LORD will rule over you."
JUDGES 8:23 NIV

It was hard for Israel to understand the lesson of Gideon's victory. God allowed only three hundred soldiers in the battle. This was for a purpose. "You would only take the glory away from me," God told them. "You'd say, 'I've saved myself by my own strength.'"

Today is like the way it was then. People still want to save themselves without God. They also want people to be their rulers and leaders, taking God's place. These are the lessons to be learned from the book of Judges. So Gideon's story ends sadly.

As soon as Gideon was dead, the Israelites began to worship other gods. They forgot the Lord, who had rescued them from their enemies. They weren't even loyal to Gideon's family. And he had done so much good for Israel. This is why Israel fell back into suffering without the care of the Lord.

Dear God, help me never to let anything take your place in my life.

ASK FOR DIRECTION

Then Manoah prayed to the LORD: "O Lord, I beg you,
let the man of God you sent to us come again to teach us how
to bring up the boy who is to be born."
JUDGES 13:8 NIV

I once worked as a canoe guide in the lakes of southern Canada. I led people on long trips into the lakes and woods. One day, I led a dozen people in four canoes into Canada. On our second morning, we were on a large lake called Basswood. As I was paddling along, I noticed trees and rocks that looked familiar. We'd passed by them a short time before. Then I realized that I didn't know where I was on that big lake. The other people had been following me all morning. I had led them around a large island several times.

Right away, we stopped for lunch. I asked for some help reading the map and compass. Soon we found our way out of Basswood. This taught me to trust the map and ask directions. This is a good way to pray. If you don't know what is going on, ask God. This is what Manoah did. He asked God for directions. This simple prayer opened the door for Manoah and his wife. They had a wonderful experience of the Lord.

Dear God, help me to ask you for directions in my life.

UNUSUAL LEADERS

The Spirit of the LORD came upon him in power so that he tore the lion
apart with his bare hands as he might have torn a young goat.
JUDGES 14:6 NIV

The judges of Israel were not elected leaders. They weren't kings or queens. Deborah was a wise woman. But still she was a woman, and Israel didn't normally have women as leaders. Gideon was cowardly. God found him hiding in a winepress. Leaders are not normally cowards. Samson was a violent man, not someone you would normally choose as your leader.

But the stories of the book of Judges are not about normal times. This is why the people in these stories aren't what you would expect.

Samson killed a young lion with his bare hands. This was as easy for him as killing a baby goat. Later, he found what was left of the lion. It was probably just a skeleton where a swarm of bees made a hive. In it, Samson found honey. He was so reckless that he grabbed the honey with his hands and ate it. So he had to face the bees. He wasn't afraid of the teeth of a lion. Why would he fear the stings of tiny bees? This is why Samson would rescue Israel from their enemies, the Philistines. "They swarmed around me like bees," says the Bible. "But I destroyed them all in the name of the Lord."

Dear God, help me to remember that when I have you, I have nothing to fear.

POWER FROM GOD

But the Spirit of the L ORD powerfully took control of Samson,
and he snapped the ropes on his arms as if they were burnt strands of flax,
and they fell from his wrists. Then he picked up a donkey's jawbone
that was lying on the ground and killed a thousand Philistines with it.
JUDGES 15:14–15 NLT

Samson caught three hundred foxes. He tied their tails together in pairs and tied a torch to each pair. Then he lit the torches and let the foxes run through the Philistines' fields. This way he burned all their grain. He also destroyed their grapevines and olive trees. Next, Samson attacked the Philistines and killed many of them. Then he went to live in a cave.

The Philistines set up camp in Judah and raided the town of Lehi. The Israelites asked the Philistines, "Why have you attacked us?"

"We've come to capture Samson. We've come to pay him back for what he did to us."

So three thousand Israelites went to get Samson at his cave. "Don't you know the Philistines rule us?" they asked him. "What are you doing to us?"

Samson replied, "I paid them back for what they did to me."

"We've come to tie you up and hand you over to the Philistines. We won't kill you." So they tied him up with two new ropes and led him away from the rock. But they didn't understand how strong the Lord had made Samson. When he got to Lehi, he killed a thousand Philistines with a mule's jawbone!

Dear God, thank you for your strength and power.

BELONGING TO GOD

Delilah lulled Samson to sleep with his head in her lap,
and she called in a man to shave off his hair,
making his capture certain.
And his strength left him.
JUDGES 16:19 NLT

Samson fell in love with a woman named Delilah, who lived in the valley of Sorek. The Philistine leaders told her, "Find out what makes Samson so strong. Then each of us will give you eleven hundred pieces of silver."

So Delilah said to Samson, "Please tell me what makes you so strong. What would it take to tie you up?"

Samson lied to her. "Tie me up with seven new bowstrings."

But that did not work, and Delilah said to him, "You made fun of me and told me a lie!"

Day after day, she nagged Samson until he couldn't stand it any longer. So he told her his secret.

"I was given to God when I was a baby. If my head is shaved, my strength will leave me. I will become as weak as anyone else."

Samson was strong because he belonged to God. The sign of this was his long hair. Like Samson, we can be strong in spirit. We simply give ourselves to God each day in prayer. Then God's enemies will have no power over us.

Dear God, help me to be strong in you.

HERO OF THE FAITH

And Samson took hold of the two middle pillars upon which the house stood. . . .
And Samson said, Let me die with the Philistines.
And he bowed himself with all his might; and the house fell.
JUDGES 16:29–30 KJV

Do you have a favorite superhero? There are so many to choose from—Superman, Batman, Spiderman, and Daredevil are just a few. Samson is not just a superhero. He carried out many heroic acts for Israel's freedom. God's Spirit was with him from beginning to end. He tore a lion apart with his bare hands! He killed a thousand men

using a donkey's jawbone! He tore the gates off the city of Gaza! By the power of the Spirit, Samson did many amazing things for Israel.

The greatest thing Samson did was the last thing he ever did. Samson's enemies had captured him and cut out his eyes. He was on display like an animal in a zoo. Had his heroic life ended in defeat?

Samson was taken into a temple to entertain his enemies. Three thousand men and women were watching. He put his hands on the pillars that held the roof of the building. "O God, please strengthen me one more time," Samson prayed. Then God enabled him to push over the pillars, and this destroyed the temple. Thousands of enemies died with Samson that day.

Samson did this to show one last time that God was with him. He died for God's people, and this makes him much more than a superhero. Samson is a hero of the faith.

Dear God, help me to be a hero of the faith like Samson.

YOUR GOD, MY GOD

Ruth replied, "Don't ask me to leave you and turn back.
I will go wherever you go and live wherever you live.
Your people will be my people, and your God will be my God."
RUTH 1:16 NLT

Ruth was in a hard situation. The three men closest to her were dead—her husband, father-in-law, and brother-in-law. Ruth was left with nothing. So she began walking to Israel with her mother-in-law, Naomi, and her sister-in law, Orpah. In those days, a woman's husband owned everything. A woman had no property or civil rights. If the husband died, the wife was cast away and could never be married again. Ruth knew her situation was bad. She said, "I will die where you die and will be buried there."

Ruth made a good decision, though her life looked hopeless. She told Naomi, "I will go wherever you go and live wherever you live. Your people will be my people, and your God will be my God." This is a decision each of us must make. If your life is easy or hard, you can choose God. Your father, mother, or a friend may be a believer in Jesus. One of them can guide you to know the Lord. Simply say what Ruth told Naomi: "Your people will be my people, and your God will be my God."

Dear God, I want you to be my God.

SHELTER IN GOD

And Ruth the Moabitess said to Naomi, "Let me go to the fields and pick up the leftover grain behind anyone in whose eyes I find favor."
RUTH 2:2 NIV

Ruth was very poor. You can see this in the way she got her food. She gleaned behind the reapers—the people who cut grain used to make bread. To glean means to gather up the leftovers. In those days, reapers left some grain at the edges of the fields. Some grain

dropped along the way. A gleaner picked up this unwanted grain. Today, some very poor people search through Dumpsters for food that has been thrown away. They could also be called gleaners.

Poor Ruth. She was young and unwanted. Her husband was dead, and she ate what others didn't want. She had only one thing going for her. She had attached herself to Naomi—a child of Israel and a believer in God.

Naomi was the mother of Ruth's husband. There in Israel, she had a relative named Boaz. Ruth happened to be gleaning in Boaz's barley field. Boaz fell in love with Ruth and began to take care of her. This was his blessing to her: "May the Lord, the God of Israel, under whose wings you have come to take refuge, reward you fully."

This blessing comes to people who seek shelter in God.

Dear God, thank you for blessing people who seek help from you.

RUTH'S BABY

So Boaz took Ruth and she became his wife.
And the LORD enabled her to conceive,
and she gave birth to a son.

RUTH 4:13 NIV

The book of Ruth tells the Bible's best love story. Boaz loved Ruth. He married her and took her to his home to live with him. Soon, Ruth had a baby—a little boy.

The women in town said to Naomi, "Praise the Lord! May this child restore your youth and care for you in your old age." Naomi took care of the baby and cared for him as if he were her own. All the townsfolk said, "Now Naomi has a son again!"

The love of Boaz and Ruth was a part of God's plan. Their son, Obed, became the father of Jesse and the grandfather of David, the king of Israel. But this is not the end of the story.

Ruth was not born in Israel; she was from a place called Moab. The Moabites were enemies of Israel. Ruth's first husband was an Israelite. After he died, she came to Israel with Naomi who was her husband's mother. There she met Boaz, her second husband.

Do you see? This woman Ruth was born among Israel's enemies. But she believed in the Lord. She was married twice. But she became the great grandmother of David, the king of Israel, and matriarch of Jesus Christ.

Dear God, thank you that nothing happens outside of your plan.

ANSWERED PRAYER

In bitterness of soul Hannah wept much and prayed to the LORD.
And she made a vow, saying, "O LORD Almighty, if you will only look upon
your servant's misery and remember me, and not forget your servant
but give her a son, then I will give him to the LORD for all the days of his life,
and no razor will ever be used on his head."

1 SAMUEL 1:10–13 NIV

This is the story of Hannah. She was one of two wives of a man named Elkanah. His other wife had several children and teased Hannah because she had no child. But Elkanah told Hannah that he loved her the best. But she still wept and wouldn't eat because she couldn't have a baby.

Hannah visited Shiloh to worship God. Hannah was so sad that she prayed to God in tears. She prayed for a baby boy and promised to give him to God. God's high priest, who was named Eli, saw Hannah praying. He thought she was just talking to herself.

Hannah told him, "I'm very sad and am praying to the Lord."

Eli said, "Go in peace. Israel's God will answer your prayer."

She then went away and ate a meal. She wasn't sad anymore.

The story goes on to tell how Hannah had a baby named Samuel. When he was old enough, she brought him back to Shiloh. Just as she'd promised, Hannah gave Samuel to Eli to serve God. She did this because she was so thankful that God had answered her prayer.

Dear God, thank you for answering my prayers.

SPEAK, LORD

The LORD came and stood there, calling as at the other times, "Samuel! Samuel!"
Then Samuel said, "Speak, for your servant is listening."
1 SAMUEL 3:10 NIV

Samuel had no idea that God was calling to him. He was Hannah's son and the young servant of Eli, the high priest. Three times he heard his name, "Samuel, Samuel." But he thought it was Eli calling. He was used to the high priest calling him.

Then God tried a fourth time. And then the boy answered God.

Samuel didn't know the Lord yet. He'd never heard the Lord's words. Still, he said to God, "Speak, for your servant is listening."

If you want to know the Lord, pray like Samuel: "Speak, for your servant hears." This won't happen to you right away. It will take some time.

Samuel heard God call his name three times. Finally, he just lay still in his bed and listened. Samuel's bed was tucked away somewhere in the tabernacle. God went to him there. The Bible says, "The Lord came, and stood, and called." Samuel was quiet. He was at rest. Faith in God gives us a quiet spirit like Samuel's. Then we can pray, "Speak, for your servant is listening."

Dear God, help me to listen when you speak to me.

GIVE US A KING

Finally, the leaders of Israel met at Ramah to discuss the matter with Samuel.
"Look," they told him, "you are now old, and your sons are not like you.
Give us a king like all the other nations have."

1 SAMUEL 8:4–5 NLT

Israel already had a king. It was God. Their problem was that they couldn't see God. All they could see was rumpled old Samuel, who spoke for God. He also spoke *with* God and saw heavenly things. Israel's elders only saw outward, earthly things. Samuel looked unworthy to them. "Who wants a poor old prophet?" they asked. "A king in a purple robe with guards and officers would look great!"

They should have known how blessed they were. God was near to them and heard them when they called. Still they begged, "Give us a king!" But if they had a king, Israel would be like the nearby nations who had kings but did not have God.

Today we have Jesus Christ. He is our Lord and King. Still, all around us are people who want to be our King. Let's remember how Israel, long ago, wanted a king instead of God. Then we can hold on to our King Jesus. Earthly kings will not take us away from him.

Dear God, thank you for the King of kings!

SAMUEL'S WARNING

But when they said, "Give us a king to lead us," this displeased Samuel;
so he prayed to the LORD. And the LORD told him:
"Listen to all that the people are saying to you;
it is not you they have rejected,
but they have rejected me as their king."

1 SAMUEL 8:6–7 NIV

God told Samuel to tell Israel what kind of king they would get.

"This is how such a king will treat you," Samuel told them. "He will take your sons into his army and make them run with his chariots. Some will command his troops; others will be slaves. Some will have to plow his fields and harvest his crops; others will make his weapons and chariots. The king will take your daughters from you. He'll force them to cook, bake, and make perfumes for him. He'll take away your best fields, vineyards, and olive groves. He'll take a tenth part of your harvest and give it to his officers. He'll want your slaves and demand your best cattle and donkeys. He'll demand a tenth of your flocks, and you will be his slaves. When this happens, you'll beg this king to stop. And the Lord won't help you."

The people of Israel refused to listen to Samuel's warning. "We still want a king," they said. "We want to be like the nations around us. Our king will govern us and lead us into battle."

Dear God, thank you for your warnings. Help me to listen to them.

OUTWARD APPEARANCE

There was a Benjamite, a man of standing, whose name was Kish. . . .
He had a son named Saul, an impressive young man without equal
among the Israelites—a head taller than any of the others.
1 SAMUEL 9:1–2 NIV

Israel's new king was named Saul. He was a good-looking man from a good family. The Bible doesn't tell us if he was wise or good. It doesn't say he was educated or godly. At first, we know nothing about his mind or his heart.

But we do know Saul was a tall, proper, handsome man. He had a good face and a good, graceful body. None of the children of Israel were more handsome than Saul. It seemed that he was meant to have power. Saul stood head and shoulders above everyone. He could surely fight the giant Philistine warriors.

Saul was much different than the king whom God would later choose for them. The Lord doesn't make decisions the way we do. People judge by outward looks, but the Lord looks at a person's heart. Even though Saul was tall and good-looking, in his heart, he was weak.

Saul was the kind of person the people wanted. They wanted a noble and grand king. If nothing else, at least he would look great. So Israel would have what they wanted—a king like the kings of the nations that surrounded them. This would make them just like those nations.

Dear God, thank you for looking at my heart instead of my outward appearance.

HONEST WORSHIP

Then Samuel called upon the Lord,
and that same day the LORD sent thunder and rain.
So all the people stood in awe of the LORD and of Samuel.
1 SAMUEL 12:18 NIV

Samuel had served the Lord since he was a boy. He retired as an old man, and the Israelites still didn't understand why God was unhappy about their king.

The old prophet, Samuel, stood to say farewell. It was during the wheat harvest—a dry time of year. But Samuel called to the Lord to send rain. This rain ruined the harvest.

"Pray to God for us, or we'll die!" the Israelites cried to Samuel. "We have added to our sins by asking for a king."

"Don't be afraid," Samuel said to comfort them. "You have done wrong. Now, make sure you worship the Lord with all your heart. Never turn your back on him again. Don't go back to worshiping idols. They cannot rescue you. They are useless! The Lord won't throw you away. This would dishonor his great name. He made you his special nation."

"You can be sure I won't sin by not praying for you. And I'll keep teaching you what is good and right. Just be sure to fear and honestly worship the Lord. Think of all the wonderful things he has done for you. But be warned: If you continue to sin, you and your king will be destroyed."

Dear God, help me to worship you with all my heart. Help me not to turn my back on you.

MORE THAN A BODY

The LORD said to Samuel, "How long will you mourn for Saul,
since I have rejected him as king over Israel? . . .
I am sending you to Jesse of Bethlehem.
I have chosen one of his sons to be king."

1 SAMUEL 16:1 NIV

Samuel was always sorry about Saul. The Lord was, too. God wished that Saul were not king of Israel. So the Lord sent Samuel to find a new king.

"How can I make someone else king?" Samuel asked God. "If Saul hears about it, he'll kill me."

Still, Samuel did as the Lord said. He arrived at Bethlehem and said, "I've come to sacrifice to the Lord. Come with me." A man named Jesse and his sons were there.

Samuel took one look at Jesse's oldest son. "This must be the new king!" he thought.

But the Lord said to Samuel, "Don't look at how handsome he is. He's not the one. I don't do things the way you do. People only see how people look. The Lord sees a person's heart."

When I was a boy, we played baseball. I remember dry Colorado days on a dusty playground. There we would choose sides for the ball game. Of course, everyone wanted the best players on their team. The strongest, the tallest, and the fastest players were always picked first.

This is fine for sandlot baseball. But God does not do things this way. Remember, a person is more than his body. He also has a soul and a spirit.

Dear God, thank you for making me special on the outside and the inside.

KiNG DAViD

But Samuel said to Jesse, "The Lord has not chosen any of these."
Then Samuel asked, "Are these all the sons you have?"
"There is still the youngest," Jesse replied.
"But he's out in the fields watching the sheep."

1 SAMUEL 16:10—11 NLT

Jesse told his son, Abinadab, to walk in front of Samuel. But Samuel knew he was not the one to be king. The same was true of Shammah. In fact, Samuel told Jesse that none of his seven sons would be king.

Samuel may have wondered why he was there. But, he happened to ask Jesse, "Are these all the sons you have?"

Jesse replied, "The youngest is out in the fields watching the sheep."

I wonder why the youngest son wasn't there in the first place. Maybe even his own father didn't think he could be king.

"Send for him right now," Samuel said. "We won't eat until he gets here."

So Jesse sent for David. He was healthy and handsome with pleasant eyes.

The Lord said, "This is the one."

David stood there among his brothers. Samuel took olive oil and poured it on David's head. This made him king, even though he was little more than a boy. The Lord's Spirit was with David from that day on.

Even though his own father wouldn't have believed it, David was the king.

Dear God, thank you for giving David your Spirit. Thank you for choosing him to become the king.

BIG TROUBLE

A champion named Goliath, who was from Gath,
came out of the Philistine camp. He was over nine feet tall.
1 SAMUEL 17:4 NIV

Goliath was the champion of the army of the Philistines. He was a giant of a man—over nine feet tall! He wore a bronze helmet. His coat of mail weighed 125 pounds. He also had bronze leggings, and

he slung a bronze javelin over his back. The shaft of his spear was heavy and thick. Its tip was an iron spearhead that weighed fifteen pounds. Goliath walked toward the army of Israel. His servant went ahead of him carrying a huge shield.

The giant stood in the valley and shouted, "Do you need a whole army to fight us? Choose someone to fight for you, and I will fight for the Philistines. The two of us will solve this problem. If your man can kill me, we'll be your slaves. But if I kill him, you'll be our slaves! I dare you! Send a man who will fight with me!"

Saul and the Israelites heard this, and they were scared stiff. But remember what we've learned about King David. People judge by outward looks. The Lord looks at a person's heart. Goliath looked terrible. Who could fight a man nine feet tall? No one could imagine this. But, with faith in God, there was a way.

Dear God, thank you that nothing is too big for you to handle.

SEEING AS GOD SEES

David was the youngest. The three oldest followed Saul,
but David went back and forth from Saul to tend his father's sheep at Bethlehem.
1 SAMUEL 17:14–15 NIV

David was still in the field looking after the sheep. His big brothers were at the battleground. Meanwhile, twice a day for forty days, the gigantic Goliath strutted in front of the Israelite army.

One day Jesse said to David, "Take this roasted grain and these loaves of bread to your brothers. See how they are doing, and bring me back a letter from them."

So David set out with the gifts. As he arrived at the edge of the camp the Israelite army was leaving for the battlefield. He heard shouts and battle cries. David hurried to greet his brothers. As he was talking with them, he saw Goliath challenge the army of Israel.

The Israelite army ran away in fright. "Have you seen the giant?" they asked. "Have you heard about the huge reward offered to anyone who kills him? The king will give one of his daughters for a wife. The man's whole family will be exempted from paying taxes!"

David wondered, "Who is this pagan Philistine anyway? How can we allow him to defy the armies of the living God?"

Saul and all of Israel's soldiers only saw the gigantic size of Goliath. But David saw as God saw, and he had faith.

Dear God, help me to see things like you see them.

FAITH IN GOD'S POWER

"Don't worry about a thing," David told Saul.
"I'll go fight this Philistine!"
1 SAMUEL 17:32 NLT

David said a very bold thing, "Who is this Philistine? How can we allow him to defy God's army?" Right away, word got back to Saul, who was sure David couldn't fight Goliath.

But David didn't give up. "I take care of my father's sheep," he said. "If a wild animal tries steal a lamb, I go after it with a club. If the animal turns on me, I kill it. I've done this to lions and bears. I'll do it to this Philistine, too. He's challenged the armies of the living God! The Lord saved me from the claws of the lion and the bear. God will save me from Goliath, too!"

"All right, go ahead," Saul said. "May the Lord be with you!"

Saul gave David his armor. David put it on and strapped on the sword. He took a step or two to see what it was like. "I can't go in these," he said. "I'm not used to them." So he took them off. He didn't trust in Saul's armor.

David picked up five smooth stones from a stream. Then, with only his shepherd's staff and sling, he started across to fight Goliath. He was trusting God.

Dear God, help me to have faith in your power, just like David did.

DAVID BEATS GOLIATH!

He picked up five smooth stones from a stream and put them in his shepherd's bag.
Then, armed only with his shepherd's staff and sling,
he started across to fight Goliath.
1 SAMUEL 17:40 NLT

Young David did something no man in Israel dared to do. He went out to fight the giant Goliath. He could do this because of his strong faith in God.

"Come over here," Goliath yelled. "I'll feed your flesh to the birds and wild animals!"

"You come to me with your sword and spear," David shouted back. "I come to you in the name of the Almighty. Today the God of Israel will conquer you. I'll kill you and cut off your head. Then I'll give the dead bodies of your men to the wild animals. The whole world will know that there is a God in Israel! The Lord doesn't need weapons to rescue his people. It's his battle, not ours. The Lord will give you to us!"

Goliath moved closer to attack. David quickly ran out to meet him. He reached into his shepherd's bag and took out a stone. He hurled the stone from his sling and hit the Philistine in the forehead. The stone sank in. Goliath stumbled and fell face down on the ground.

David killed Goliath with only a stone and sling. He pulled Goliath's sword from its sheath and cut off the giant's head.

Dear God, thank you that no battle is too difficult for you.

JEALOUSY

Whatever Saul asked David to do, David did it successfully.
So Saul made him a commander in his army,
an appointment that was applauded by the fighting men and officers alike.
1 SAMUEL 18:5 NLT

When Israel's army returned home after David had killed Goliath, women came out from all the towns along the way to celebrate and to cheer for King Saul. They sang and danced for joy with tambourines and cymbals. This was their song: "Saul has killed his thousands and David his ten thousands!"

The song made Saul angry. "What's this?" he said. "They say David killed ten thousands and me only thousands. Next they'll make him their king!" So from that time on, Saul was jealous of David.

The very next day, Saul was in pain in his spirit. He began to rave like a madman. Whenever this happened, David played the harp for the king. But this time, Saul had a spear in his hand. Suddenly he threw it at David, trying to pin him to the wall. But David jumped aside and escaped.

This had happened before. Saul was afraid and jealous of David. He knew the Lord had left him behind and was now with David. Finally, Saul refused to see David. He made him commander over only a thousand men. But David didn't fight with Saul. Instead, he faithfully led his troops into battle.

Dear God, help me not to be jealous like Saul. Help me to be faithful like David.

RESPECT FOR AUTHORITY

"It is a serious thing to attack the LORD's anointed one,
for the LORD himself has chosen him."
So David sharply rebuked his men and did not let them kill Saul.

1 SAMUEL 24:6–7 NLT

As you now know, King Saul was jealous of David. In fact, he wanted to kill the young man. Once, Saul returned from battle and learned David had gone into the wilderness. So, choosing three thousand soldiers, Saul went to search for David and his men. At the place where the road passed some sheepfolds, there was a cave. Saul went into that cave. But it just so happened that David and his men were hiding there!

"Now's your chance!" David's men whispered to him. "Remember, the Lord said, 'I will put Saul into your power, to do with as you wish.'" Then David crept forward and cut off a piece of Saul's robe.

David's conscience bothered him because he had cut Saul's robe. "The Lord knows I shouldn't have done that," he said to his men. "It is a serious thing to attack the Lord's king." So David did not let his men kill Saul.

Then Saul left the cave and went on his way. David came out and shouted after him, "My lord the king!" When Saul looked around, David bowed low before him. Even though Saul hated him, David still respected his king.

Dear God, help me to respect my authorities like you've asked me to do.

GOOD FOR EVIL

And he said to David, "You are a better man than I am,
for you have repaid me good for evil."
1 SAMUEL 24:17 NLT

Has anyone ever treated you badly? Maybe someone bullied you at school or lied about you. David shows how to act toward such people. Saul wasn't just a bully, and he wasn't telling lies about David—he was trying to kill him!

David told Saul, "Look at what I have in my hand. It's a piece of your robe! I cut it off, but I didn't kill you. This proves I'm not trying to harm you."

Then David reminded Saul of an old proverb. "From evil people come evil deeds," he said. "So you can be sure I will never harm you."

Saul called back, "Is that really you, David?" Then he began to cry. "You're a better man than I am. I gave you evil and you repaid me with good. Yes, you have been wonderfully kind to me today. You could have killed me but you didn't do it. I hope the Lord will reward you for your kindness toward me. Now I know you're going to be king. So pledge this to me: When you're king, you won't kill my family!"

David promised this and Saul went home. But David and his men went back to their fort.

Dear God, help me to be kind even when others are not being kind to me.

TRUE GREATNESS

Nathan replied to the king,
"Whatever you have in mind, go ahead and do it,
for the LORD is with you."

2 SAMUEL 7:3 NIV

David, the king of Israel, will always be remembered. God chose him to lead Israel when he was just a shepherd boy. The Lord was with David wherever he went and destroyed all his enemies. Because of David, God made a homeland for Israel, and there they were safe from all their enemies.

This was God's promise to David: "I will set up the throne of your kingdom forever. It will continue for all time and will stay forever." God made David's name famous all over the earth. David's sons were always to be the kings of Israel. His son Solomon made the kingdom of Israel a world power. He also built a beautiful temple for God.

The Bible tells many famous stories about David. Almost everyone knows about David and Goliath. But David is most important because Jesus Christ came out of his family. The Bible even says that Jesus is "the son of David."

It is interesting to read about David. When you do, remember that God had a reason for David's life. He was great because the things he did made it possible for Jesus to be born.

Dear God, please do great things through my life, just as you did through David's.

SEEKING WISDOM

*"Give me an understanding mind so that I can govern your people well
and know the difference between right and wrong."*

1 KINGS 3:9 NLT

Solomon was the first of David's family to become the king of Israel. One night, the Lord appeared to him in a dream and said, "What do you want? Ask me for it and I'll give it to you."

"I'm like a little child," prayed Solomon. "And here I am, the king of your chosen people. All I ask is that you give me wisdom. With it, I can rule your people well. I can know the difference between right and wrong. No one can govern your great nation alone."

The Lord liked Solomon's prayer and was glad he'd asked for wisdom. He replied, "You've asked for wisdom in governing my people. You haven't asked for a long life, riches, or the death of your enemies. So I'll give you what you asked for—a wise and understanding mind. No one else has ever had such wisdom before or ever will again! I'll also give you what you did not ask for—riches and honor! No other king in the world will be like you. Plus, if you follow and obey me like David did, I'll give you a long life."

That is why Solomon became such a wise and good king.

Dear God, help me to ask you for the things I need, and please bless me according to your will.

TWO WOMEN AND A BABY

Word of the king's decision spread quickly throughout all Israel, and the people were awed as they realized the great wisdom God had given him.

1 KINGS 3:28 NLT

One day, two women came to Solomon with an argument. One of them began, "This woman and I live together. I gave birth to a baby, and three days later she did, too. But her baby died during the night because she rolled over on it. Then she got up and took my son from me while I was asleep. She put her dead child in my arms and took mine to sleep beside her. In the morning, my son was dead! Then I saw that it wasn't my son at all!"

The other woman broke in, "The living child is mine."

"No," the first woman said, "the living one is mine."

Then King Solomon said, "Cut the living child in two and give half to each woman!"

The woman who really was the mother of the living child loved him very much. She cried out, "Oh no! Give her the child—please do not kill him!"

Then the king said, "Don't kill him. Give the baby to the woman who wants him to live. She is his mother!"

People were awed at the great wisdom God had given to Solomon.

Dear God, please give me your wisdom to know what is right and what is wrong.

NEED WISDOM? ASK!

When the queen of Sheba realized how wise Solomon was,
and when she saw the palace he had built, she was breathless.
1 KINGS 10:4–5 NLT

The queen of Sheba was from a faraway land. There she heard of Solomon, the king of Israel, and his wisdom. She came to see him and test him with hard questions. Picture this beautiful woman riding into Jerusalem with a long camel train. The camels carried rare spices, gold, and precious stones as gifts for the king. The queen talked with Solomon about everything on her mind. Solomon answered all her questions.

The queen of Sheba saw Solomon's wisdom. She said to him, "What I heard about you was true. You have great wisdom. I didn't believe it until I came and saw it with my own eyes. Your wisdom is greater than what I was told."

Where did Solomon get his wisdom? He asked God for it. "Give me an understanding mind so that I can govern your people well and know the difference between right and wrong," he prayed.

Anyone can have wisdom. All you need to do is ask for it. The Bible says, "If you need wisdom—if you want to know what God wants you to do—ask him, and he will gladly tell you."

Dear God, help me to remember that all wisdom comes from you.

MEET ELIJAH

Then the woman told Elijah,
"Now I know for sure that you are a man of God,
and that the LORD truly speaks through you."
1 KINGS 17:24 NLT

The Bible is a book of names. It mentions thousands of people. So far, you have read the names of many famous people. These may be among the most famous in the world. Adam and Eve came first with their sons Cain and Abel. Then there were Abraham and Sarah, their son Isaac, and grandson Jacob. Jacob's twelve sons are known as the sons of Israel. Their families are the children of Israel, the Jewish race. Moses rescued this great nation from Egypt and brought them to the Promised Land.

You've also read of Deborah and Samson, brave judges of Israel; the boy-prophet Samuel; and Saul, the failed king of Israel. Now you know of David, Israel's shepherd-king and his wise son Solomon. Next, you'll learn of Israel's greatest prophet, Elijah.

All these people believed and hoped in God. In this way, they were like you and me. We also believe in the Lord.

Dear God, thank you for telling me about your great people. Help me to be great for you, too.

A STILL, SMALL VOICE

"Go out and stand before me on the mountain," the LORD *told him.*
And as Elijah stood there, the LORD *passed by.*
1 KINGS 19:11 NLT

This is a gentle conversation between God and Elijah. I don't know of anything like it since God spoke with Adam. In those days, in Eden, God would walk in the garden. Here, it is different. Elijah is hiding in a cave on a mountain in a terrible desert.

The Lord told Elijah, "Go out and stand in front of me on the mountain."

As Elijah stood there, the Lord passed by and a windstorm hit. It was so terrible that the rocks were torn from the mountain! But the Lord wasn't in the wind. Then there was an earthquake, but the Lord wasn't in the earthquake. After the earthquake, there was a fire. The Lord wasn't in the fire, either. Finally, Elijah heard a still, small voice. Wrapped in his cloak, Elijah stood outside the cave. There, the voice said, "What are you doing here, Elijah?"

Wind, earthquake, and fire had come upon Elijah, but God wasn't in them. Instead, God was in a tiny voice that could hardly be heard. Many people think of God as awesome and powerful, and He is. But God also comes to us in small ways that we need not fear. The best and most loving way was a baby named Jesus Christ.

Dear God, thank you for showing yourself to us in big and small ways.

YOU'RE NOT ALONE

"Yet I will preserve seven thousand others in Israel
who have never bowed to Baal or kissed him!"

1 KINGS 19:18 NLT

By the cave on the mountain, Elijah heard God's gentle voice say, "What are you doing here?"

Elijah answered, "The people of Israel have broken their promises to you. They've torn down your altars and killed every one of your prophets. Only I am left, and now they're trying to kill me, too."

If you love the Lord, on some days you may feel like Elijah. Around him were wind, earthquake, and fire. He was in danger. Some people may say that God is in such things, but Elijah knew better. So he listened and heard God's quiet voice. This comforted him.

Elijah felt like he was alone. He thought, "I'm the only one in Israel who loves the Lord." It is easy to feel that no one else cares for God. But Elijah learned that this is not true.

God told him, "I will protect seven thousand people in Israel who have never bowed to Baal or kissed him!" Baal was a so-called god that was worshiped in the days of Elijah. Today, most people love many things, but not God. But just as it was when Elijah lived, God still has many true believers in this world. Pray, and you will find them.

Dear God, help me to know other people who love you, too.

ELIJAH'S END

As they were walking along and talking, suddenly a chariot of fire appeared,
drawn by horses of fire. It drove between them, separating them,
and Elijah was carried by a whirlwind into heaven.

2 KINGS 2:11 NLT

Everyone who is born must die. But Elijah didn't.

Elijah had a follower named Elisha. As they walked together, Elijah said to Elisha, "The Lord has told me to go to the Jordan River. You stay here."

But Elisha told him, "I will never leave you."

The two stopped beside the Jordan River. Elijah folded his

cloak together and hit the water with it. The river divided, and they went across on dry ground.

On other side, Elijah said to Elisha, "What can I do for you before I am taken away?"

"Please let me have twice the amount of your spirit," Elisha answered.

"That's a hard thing," said Elijah. "If you see me when I am taken away, then you'll get it. But if not, then you won't."

Suddenly, there was a chariot of fire pulled by horses of fire. It drove between the two men and Elijah was carried into heaven by a whirlwind. Elisha saw it and cried out, "My father! My father! The chariots and horsemen of Israel!"

Then Elisha picked up Elijah's cloak and struck the river with it. He cried out, "Where is the Lord, the God of Elijah?" Then the river divided, and Elisha went back across.

Dear God, help me to see your miracles, just like Elisha did.

SHOWING GOD TO THE WORLD

When Elisha reached the house, there was the boy lying dead on his couch.
He went in, shut the door on the two of them and prayed to the LORD.
2 KINGS 4:32–33 NIV

As you read the Bible, you'll find many people like Elisha. They did miracles and told of the future to show God's power in this world. These people usually lived in times when God's people were weak in the faith. In times like those, believers didn't live in ways that showed the Lord. Because of this, the world didn't know about God. So prophets like Elisha came along to show God to the world.

Elisha was the helper and student of Elijah, who was Israel's greatest prophet. When God took Elijah away to heaven in a whirlwind, Elisha became the leader of Israel's prophets.

Elisha lived about 2,900 years ago, served God for sixty years, and did amazing things. He changed poisoned water into a clean spring. He supplied water to Israel's thirsty army. He increased a poor widow's supply of oil. He brought life back to a woman's dead son. He made twenty loaves of bread into enough to feed one hundred men. He cured the leader of Syria's army from leprosy. And he made an iron ax head float.

But remember, Elisha didn't do these things to make himself famous. He did miracles so the world would know God.

Dear God, help me to live my life so that others will come to know you.

SICK WITH PRIDE

But though Naaman was a mighty warrior,
he suffered from leprosy.
2 KINGS 5:1 NLT

This man Naaman was powerful and desperate. He was the commander of the Syrian army. He was also a leper. This means he suffered from an incurable disease of the skin called leprosy. Naaman heard of a prophet in Israel who could cure him. So he went to Israel to find Elisha the prophet. When he found him, he was told to wash in the Jordan River seven times. This made Naaman furious.

Naaman was an important man! He'd come to Israel with all his followers carrying hundreds of pounds of silver and gold. He arrived at Elisha's poor little house expecting more than he got. Naaman expected Elisha to come out of his house. But Elisha's servant came out instead. Naaman wanted Elisha to say some magic words. He expected a sacrifice to God and some soothing ointment for the leprosy. Instead, he was told to wash in the ordinary water of the Jordan River. Naaman was too proud to do this.

The same is true today. People are sick in their souls. They don't have leprosy, but they have sin. And they are too proud for the simple remedy of faith. This cure seems too simple. But it is God's way. Faith in Jesus is the only cure for sin.

Dear God, help me not to be prideful.

EYES OF FAITH

"For we have no power to face this vast army that is attacking us.
We do not know what to do, but our eyes are upon you."

2 CHRONICLES 20:12 NIV

Did you ever hear the saying, "Seeing is believing"? We say this because we use our eyes to find our way in this world. In 2 Chronicles, King Jehoshaphat said, "Our eyes are upon you." He was looking at God and believing.

Jehoshaphat and his city, Jerusalem, were faced with thousands of enemy soldiers. They were powerless against them, so Jehoshaphat prayed to God. In the end he told the Lord, "Our eyes are upon you." This means that Jehoshaphat's leader was God. Soldiers in battle always keep their eyes on their leader. He is the one who knows the battle plan. If soldiers lose touch with their leaders, the battle is lost.

How can you see God? Isn't the Lord invisible? Yes, but we use the eyes of faith to see God just like Jehoshaphat did. Our eyes of faith are open when we pray to God, and then we can see and believe him.

Dear God, thank you for letting me see and believe you.

JOB

There was a man named Job who lived in the land of Uz.
He was blameless, a man of complete integrity.
He feared God and stayed away from evil.

JOB 1:1 NLT

The man named Job had a good life. He had seven sons and three daughters and many animals—seven thousand sheep, three thousand camels, five hundred teams of oxen, and five hundred female donkeys. God thought he was the finest man in the land. He was honest and honorable. He loved God and had nothing to do with evil. But he lost all he had in one day.

Job may have planned his life carefully. He worked hard to get what he wanted. But God had other plans for him. When he lost everything, Job's wife told him to curse God and die. Job answered, "Should we accept only good things from the hand of God and never anything bad?"

Job's story shows that we can't know the future. A man once said, "Listen to me. You say, 'I'm going away for a year. I'm going to do some business and make good money.' How do you know what will happen tomorrow? Your life is like the morning fog. It's here a little while and then it's gone."

I don't think this means we shouldn't make plans. It means we should be humble. We should know that God controls everything, including our lives.

Dear God, thank you for all the good things in my life. Help me to deal with the bad.

PRAYER AND PEACE

So many are saying, "God will never rescue him!"
But you, O LORD, are a shield around me, my glory,
and the one who lifts my head high.

PSALM 3:2–3 NLT

This is a song by David, the king of Israel. At the time, his own son, Absalom, was hunting him down. Absalom rebelled against his father. He even tried to kill him and take over the throne of Israel.

Things were so bad for David that people said not even God could help him. But nothing is impossible for God. He can always help. David found help in God, and so can we.

David said, "O Lord, you are my shield and my glory, the one who lifts my head high." He prayed, crying out loud to the Lord, and he knew that God heard him. His faith made him sure of this. What great hope we have that God hears our prayers!

Prayer gave David real peace. This is why he tells of how soundly he could sleep, despite his troubles. "I lay down and slept," he said. "I woke up in safety, for the Lord was watching over me." David made his requests known to God, and his heart and mind were kept by God's peace.

Dear God, please give me the same peace King David had by trusting in you.

NATURE TELLS ABOUT GOD

The heavens tell of the glory of God.
The skies display his marvelous craftsmanship.
Day after day they continue to speak;
night after night they make him known.
PSALM 19:1–2 NLT

Do you want to know God? Is there someone you love who you hope will believe in God? Here is an easy way to see God. The heavens announce God's glory. The skies shout about the work of his hands.

This has been happening since the fourth day of Creation, when God said, "Let bright lights appear in the sky." Since then, they continue to speak about God day after day. Night after night, they make him known. If only people would pay attention! It doesn't matter where you are from or what language you speak. Nature tells all about God. Yes, God is invisible. But the Bible says that God and all of his power can be seen through nature.

Many people pray that their family and friends will be open to God. They want them to believe in Jesus Christ. We hope they will hear the gospel. God's Creation is the greatest preacher of all. Let's pray that everyone will see it and believe it!

Dear God, help me to open my eyes every day to see your wonderful Creation.

GOD IS ON YOUR SIDE

You keep track of all my sorrows.
You have collected all my tears in your bottle.
You have recorded each one in your book.
On the very day I call to you for help, my enemies will retreat.
This I know: God is on my side.

PSALM 56:8—9 NLT

Your father cares for you in many ways. He gives you food, clothing, and a warm house. He thinks about your health, too. He worries about your schoolwork, and he likes to watch you play. Sometimes he has to correct you, too. Has your father ever gotten angry? This may be because he cares so much for you. After all his years of caring, I hope you will say, "My dad is on my side."

This is what David, the author of Psalm 56, said about his heavenly Father. God paid close attention to David's life. David said God counted how many times he tossed and turned in the night. His tears were collected in a bottle and counted in a book. So David could say, "This I know: God is on my side."

Like a father with his child, God cares for you and me. So we also can say, "This I know, God is on my side." God cares for us for a reason, and he has a purpose. Everything that happens is for God's plan. This is why we Christians know that God is for us. So who can be against us?

Dear God, thank you for being on my side.

OUR REAL HOME

In thee, O Lord, do I put my trust....
Be thou my strong habitation.
PSALM 71:1, 3 KJV

I used to stay at my grandparent's house when I was young. But now their house is gone, and so are my grandparents. Their house didn't last and neither did their bodies. Everything in this world is temporary.

But David prayed for a permanent home. "Be thou my strong habitation." Have you ever heard anyone pray words like these? David was saying, "O God, be my home, be my dwelling place." This means that God can be our home. This isn't a house like my grandfather's. It can't be seen, but it's real and it's strong. God is our home because we believe in God.

Other believers knew this. Abraham said he was a sojourner in the land. This means he only lived there for a little while. Moses said, "I have been a stranger in a strange land." God told the Hebrews that they were sojourners, too. Even David said this was true. In a way, they all said they were homeless. This is because they knew their real home was God.

Let's enjoy living in our houses and sleeping in our beds. But at the same time, let's pray like David. "Lord, be my permanent home where I am always safe."

Dear God, please be my permanent home where I am always safe.

HELP IN TROUBLE

I called upon the LORD in distress: the LORD answered me,
and set me in a large place.
PSALM 118:5 KJV

I once lived in a cottage by the beach. It was built of stone on the outside and wood paneling on the inside. It looked like a storybook house. When the morning fog from the Long Island Sound lifted, sunshine poured in and washed across the couch. This marked the spot that our cat, Samson, made his own.

That was a perfect place for Samson. From there, he had long, clear views of the first floor of that cottage. He felt safe because he could see so far through the house. He could also hunt because he could see anything that moved—usually houseflies!

The psalmist called on the Lord in distress. The Lord's answer was to put him in a large place. This is something like my cat's sunny couch. He had a clear view of what was around him. To us, this means that we can understand life better when we believe in God. We can see what is around us. Ask anyone who has called on the Lord in distress. They'll tell you that the Lord answered by setting them in a large place.

Dear God, thank you that I can call on you in distress.

NOTHING IS HIDDEN

O LORD, you have examined my heart and know everything about me.
You know when I sit down or stand up.
You know my every thought when far away.
PSALM 139:1–2 NLT

We Christians know that God made the sun and sky, the moon and stars, and everything else. But the writer of Psalm 139 says that God even knows when we sit down and when we stand up.

Sitting down and standing up are such little things. We do them so many times each day. Does God watch over you that closely? Yes! This is amazing! God overlooks nothing. No wonder Psalm 139 declares, "Such knowledge is too wonderful for me."

It's true. The New Testament teaches the same thing: "Nothing is hidden from God! He sees through everything."

Read further in Psalm 139 and this will be made clear. We can never escape from the Spirit or get away from God's presence. But who would want to? No matter where you are, God is there. His hand guides you and his almighty strength supports you.

Dear God, thank you for knowing everything—and everything about me.

CREATION HONORS GOD

Praise the LORD from the earth, you great sea creatures and all ocean depths,
lightning and hail, snow and clouds, stormy winds that do his bidding,
you mountains and all hills, fruit trees and all cedars, wild animals and all cattle,
small creatures and flying birds, kings of the earth and all nations,
you princes and all rulers on earth, young men and maidens,
old men and children.
PSALM 148:7–12 NIV

Our faith tells us rain comes from God. Some people laugh at this idea. After all, science says that rain happens because of air, water, and heat. That may be, but God is still the one who sends us rain.

Suppose a friend sends you a beautiful gift. As you enjoy it, someone tells you a machine in a factory made it. He doesn't understand the real beauty of the gift is the giver's heart of love. The same is true with rain. In love, God sends everyone rain. The scientific reasons for rain are not as important as God's love.

Psalm 148 says the hail, snow, and clouds should praise God. In fact, the whole creation honors God. So we must take care of his creation. We must care for all creatures and their earthly homes. We get so much from creation, like food and water and shelter. We thank God for what creation gives us and in love, offer it back.

Though snow and hail cannot really praise God, they serve us well. So we bless the God of love for them.

Dear God, thank you for everything you have created.

SPRINGTIME

"My lover said to me, 'Rise up, my beloved, my fair one, and come away.
For the winter is past, and the rain is over and gone.
The flowers are springing up, and the time of singing birds has come,
even the cooing of turtledoves."

SONG OF SONGS 2:10–12 NLT

Spring is a wonderful time. It seems right that Jesus would die and come back to life in the spring. Spring sets nature free from winter. Christ's resurrection gives all creation the hope of being set free from sin.

In the Song of Songs, a man asks his love to rise up. He wants her to join him in celebrating spring's arrival. "Get up, my love, my

fair one and come away," he says. "The winter is past and the rain is over and gone." This is like Christ. When he arose from the grave, sin's long, cold winter was over. It could not rule us any more. In resurrection, new life burst forth in the Lord's believers.

The gospel of Jesus Christ warms the cold heart. With it, people come alive like trees with springtime leaves. Wherever it is welcomed, beauty appears and joy breaks forth. Springtime is a pleasant time and so are times of faith in Christ. Anyone can rise up and come away from the world with Christ. Then, he or she is born again. Winter is past and springtime has come!

Dear God, thank you for new life in you!

WATER OF LIFE

*"Surely God is my salvation; I will trust and not be afraid. The LORD,
the LORD, is my strength and my song; he has become my salvation."
With joy you will draw water from the wells of salvation.*

ISAIAH 12:2–3 NIV

There is a beautiful Bible story about a woman who was drawing water out of the town well. There she met Jesus Christ. As they talked together, the woman didn't know that Jesus is the Savior. At the right moment, Jesus said, "I am he." This changed the woman. Suddenly, she found in her heart "a well of water springing up into everlasting life." Right away, she hurried to tell the townsfolk about Jesus.

A time comes when each of us learns who Jesus is. Then, the wells of salvation open to us. We joyously draw out the water of eternal life. The end of the Bible invites everyone to drink this water: "Whoever is thirsty, let him come; and whoever wishes, let him take the free gift of the water of life."

Each time we pray, we drink of the river of water of life. Its waters flow bright as crystal out of the throne of God and of the Lamb. "The Lord is my strength and my song; he has become my salvation," we pray, drinking of the water of life. "I will trust, and not be afraid."

Dear God, thank you for being my strength and my song. Thank you for your water of life.

WAITING FOR GOD

Yes, Lord, walking in the way of your laws, we wait for you.
ISAIAH 26:8 NIV

The Bible tells this story about serving the Lord:

Jesus and the disciples were on their way to Jerusalem. They came to Bethany where they stayed with Martha and Mary. Martha worked in the kitchen preparing a big meal for everyone. Meanwhile her sister, Mary, sat with Jesus listening to his teaching.

Martha came to Jesus and said, "Lord, my sister just sits here while I do all the work. That's not fair. Tell her to come and help me."

Jesus said to her, "Dear Martha, Mary has discovered the one important thing. I won't take that away from her."

Can you imagine Mary sitting with the Lord? She was listening to every word he said. This is how Jesus wants us to serve him— to lovingly watch and listen to him. Another Bible verse talks about this. It says, "We look to the Lord our God for his mercy, just as servants keep their eyes on their master, as a slave girl watches her mistress for the slightest signal."

One day, Jesus Christ will return. We Christians should be like Mary, listening, watching, and waiting for him.

Dear God, help me to listen, watch, and wait for you.

WATCHMEN ON THE WALLS

*O Jerusalem, I have posted watchmen on your walls; they will pray
to the LORD day and night for the fulfillment of his promises.
Take no rest, all you who pray.
Give the LORD no rest until he makes Jerusalem the object
of praise throughout the earth.*
ISAIAH 62:6–7 NLT

Policemen watch over our towns and cities. They try to make sure
that nothing bad happens to us. In ancient Israel, policemen were
called *watchmen*—because the time between sunset and sunrise was
divided into three watches. Each watch had different watchmen, so
someone had to stay up all night to watch the city and keep it safe
from enemies.

The Bible says that God has set watchmen on the walls of
Jerusalem. These are not the actual watchmen who kept an eye on
Jerusalem—they are Christians who pray. Wouldn't you like to be a
watchman like that? They don't shout that enemies are coming—
they pray to God until he makes Jerusalem a thing of praise in the
earth. That happens when Jesus comes back.

We don't have to be strong or famous to pray like this. Small
prayers are important prayers. A person who says to God, "Lord, I
love You," has said something very important. Someone who can
stop and say, "Thank you," to God has done something very special.
You could be that person!

Dear God, help me to thank you in prayer every day!

Running from God

Then Jonah prayed to the LORD his God from inside the fish.
He said, "I cried out to the LORD
in my great trouble, and he answered me."
JONAH 2:1–2 NLT

Jonah was a man who ran from God. Do you think he got very far?

God wanted Jonah to go to Nineveh and preach the gospel. Jonah didn't want to do this. Instead, he got on a boat headed away

from Nineveh. But a terrible storm blew up, and the ship's crew thought Jonah was to blame. So they tossed Jonah overboard, and a large fish swallowed him. Inside the fish, Jonah prayed to God. God answered, and after three days, the fish spit Jonah out on the shore.

Jonah was a real person with a real story. The Bible uses his story to tell about Jesus. Jesus said, "Jonah was in the belly of the great fish for three days and three nights. . . . I will be in the heart of the earth for three days and three nights." Jonah's experience inside the fish was a sign that pointed to Christ's resurrection from the dead. Jonah could never have known this. He only knew that he had disobeyed God, and so he was swallowed by a fish. But God is the great director of history—Jonah's history and your history, too.

Dear God, help me to remember that no one can run from you!

SPIRITUAL FOOD

But you, O Bethlehem Ephrathah, are only a small village in Judah.
Yet a ruler of Israel will come from you.

MICAH 5:2 NLT

Bethlehem was a tiny place. Why do you think Jesus was born there? The name Bethlehem means "the house of bread." Jesus is the bread of life. It was in the little town of Bethlehem that the bread of life came to us. That is when Bethlehem became the real house of bread.

The Bible also calls Jesus the Good Shepherd of the sheep, and we are his sheep. It's interesting that he was born in Bethlehem because it was the town of David. David was a shepherd, too, and later he became the king of Israel.

The night that Jesus was born, shepherds were in the fields outside of Bethlehem. They were guarding their sheep. Suddenly, an angel of the Lord appeared, and they were very afraid. But the angel said, "Don't be afraid! I bring you good news of great joy! The Savior has been born tonight in Bethlehem! Go there and you will find a baby wrapped up and lying in a manger."

Those shepherds went into Bethlehem, the town of King David. There they found Jesus, the Good Shepherd. He was sleeping in a manger. A manger is the place where farmers put food for their sheep and cattle. The Good Shepherd is also spiritual food for his sheep—and we are his sheep!

Dear God, thank you for sending Jesus to give his sheep the spiritual food they need.

MARY'S BABY

The virgin's name was Mary. The angel went to her and said,
"Greetings, you who are highly favored! The Lord is with you."
LUKE 1:27–28 NIV

What if you were outside, sitting on the lawn, and an angel appeared. This is what happened to Mary when she was only about fourteen years old. And the angel said to her, "Don't be frightened,

Mary, for God has decided to bless you! You will become pregnant and have a son. . . . He will be very great and will be called the Son of the Most High."

Imagine the feelings in Mary's heart at that moment! Mary wasn't a prophet or an elder in Israel. She was a very young woman. But the Son of God would become a man because of her! It's hard to understand how Jesus Christ was both God and man. But it's true. God became a man named Jesus. This didn't happen by a snap of God's fingers. Mary was pregnant with Jesus for nine months. Then she gave birth like all women do, through pain of labor.

Mary knew how important her baby Jesus would be to the world. She spoke to the angel, "Oh, how I praise the Lord. How I rejoice in God my Savior! For he took notice of his lowly servant girl, and now generation after generation will call me blessed."

Dear God, please keep me humble like Mary and let me do great things for you.

ANGELS

"Joseph, son of David," the angel said,
"do not be afraid to go ahead with your marriage to Mary. . . .
She will have a son, and you are to name him Jesus,
for he will save his people from their sins."
MATTHEW 1:20–21 NLT

You'll find angels in many Bible stories, but they don't show up very often. Only at very important times do angels appear to human beings. In the days of the New Testament, angels appeared at some very important events, like when Jesus was born and the day he died.

An angel appeared in Joseph's dream for some good reasons. One was to tell him what to name Mary's baby. He was named Jesus. This means, "God our salvation." The name *Jesus* tells the world that he is God. It also shows everyone that he is salvation. He saves people from their sins.

Another name for Mary's baby was *Immanuel.* Again, this name tells us something about the baby Jesus. When he was born, God became a human being. The meaning of the name Immanuel is, "God with us."

God is always with us, and sometimes he even send angels to be with us, too.

Dear God, thank you for sending your angels at the most important times.

THE NAME OF JESUS

"The virgin will be with child and will give birth to a son,
and they will call him Immanuel"—
which means, "God with us."
MATTHEW 1:23 NIV

"You will be with child and give birth to a son,
and you are to give him the name Jesus."
LUKE 1:31 NIV

Your name is very important. It is like a code that tells who you are

and what you've done. For example, what do you think of when you hear the name *Abraham Lincoln*? He was the man who was born in a log cabin and became president of the United States. Have you heard the name *Emily Dickinson*? This name reminds people of a woman who is famous for writing poetry.

An angel made sure that Mary and Joseph knew their baby had a name. Their child would be known as *Immanuel*. This means, "God with us." An angel told Mary to name the child *Jesus*. This means, "God is salvation."

The name of Jesus means more than we can imagine. It means that God became a man and lived a perfect life. It tells of this man's death, which brought the entire creation to God. It means that he rose from the dead.

Many people have been presidents and many have been poets. But not one person has been or ever will be who Jesus Christ is.

Dear God, thank you that no one else can be who Jesus is.

HUMBLE JESUS

That night some shepherds were in the fields
outside the village, guarding their flocks of sheep.
Suddenly, an angel of the Lord appeared among them.
LUKE 2:8–9 NLT

I wonder if the shepherds were thinking about God that night. It's possible that they were praying. Or maybe they were sleeping. Suddenly, the glory of the Lord was all around them! Those hard-working men were afraid. An angel tried to calm them down. Then all around them were thousands of angels praising God. "Glory to God in the highest heaven, and peace on earth to all whom God favors," they sang. Imagine how this amazed and scared the shepherds!

These rough shepherds had courage, though. They said to each other, "Let's go to Bethlehem and see this." So they went looking for a baby wrapped in cloths, lying in a manger.

The shepherds found Mary, Joseph, and Jesus in a humble stable because there was no room for them in the inn. The shepherds and everyone they told were amazed at what happened.

Jesus wasn't born in a beautiful palace. He wasn't famous like a movie star. He simply came to do God's work and serve others. He didn't want to be served like a king, even though he is the King of kings.

Dear God, help me to be humble like Jesus Christ.

SEEK JESUS

Wise men from eastern lands arrived in Jerusalem, asking,
"Where is the newborn king of the Jews?
We have seen his star as it arose,
and we have come to worship him."
MATTHEW 2:1–2 NLT

When Jesus was born, right away people wanted to know him. Men from far away asked, "Where is the baby called King of the Jews?" The child was very young. He'd done nothing yet as the Savior of the world. But people were seeking him already!

God created all the people who live on the earth. There is a reason for this. All people should seek after God. We should reach out for God as if we were blindfolded. He is not far from any of us, and the Bible says that we live and move and exist in God. God can't be seen in a picture on the wall, but through Jesus, he is a living person whom we can know and love.

Long ago, wise men came from far away looking for Jesus, and they found him. Since then, millions of people have also thirsted for Jesus and found him. You know what it is like to be thirsty. Your soul is thirsty for God. Seek Jesus. He will be like a drink of water to you, and your soul will never be thirsty again!

Dear God, I don't want to be thirsty any more—help me to always seek your son, Jesus!

HEROD'S LIE

Then Herod sent a private message to the wise men, asking them to come see him.
At this meeting he learned the exact time when they first saw the star.
Then he told them, "Go to Bethlehem and search carefully for the child.
And when you find him, come back and tell me
so that I can go and worship him, too!"

MATTHEW 2:7–8 NLT

Herod was the king of the country where the Jews lived. Today that area is the nation of Israel. But Herod wasn't a Jew. The wise men went to Herod to learn where they could find the baby Jesus. They did this because they thought the king would know everything about Israel.

Herod knew nothing about Jesus, but he pretended that he wanted to worship the new king of the Jews. The truth was that he wanted to kill the newborn baby. Why would he do this? Because he was afraid that Jesus would take away his kingdom.

Herod said he wanted to worship Jesus, but he lied. What he really wanted was power over Israel.

Jesus once said, "You will know them by their fruits." It doesn't matter what people say. What really matters is what they do. This tells us if they really believe in Jesus.

Dear God, help me to do the things that show I believe in Jesus.

THE STAR

Once again the star appeared to them, guiding them to Bethlehem. . . .
When they saw the star, they were filled with joy!
MATTHEW 2:9–10 NLT

No one knows what the star of the wise men was. Scientists have studied long and hard to discover it. Historians have tried to find it in history. Scholars study the Bible to find it. But no one can learn

anything about it. Still, this star has special meaning to people who believe in Jesus.

The star guided the wise men from far away all the way to Israel. Then they went to see Herod. When the wise men finally left Herod's palace, they saw the star again. They were overwhelmed with joy. This might mean they had lost the star when they were with Herod. Maybe they were afraid they would never find it again. So when they saw the star again, they rejoiced!

The wise men went to Herod and couldn't see the star. How can you know if someone loves Jesus? They shine just like the wise men's star. But you can't see this shining with your eyes. It is an inner glow of love for God. If you have that love, you'll see it shine in others who love the Lord, too.

Dear God, help me to shine for you, and help me to see you shine in others, too.

CHRISTMAS PRESENTS

Then they opened their treasure chests
and gave him gifts of gold, frankincense, and myrrh.
MATTHEW 2:11 NLT

The wise men were expecting to see a newborn king. What they found was a baby who seemed to be just the son of an ordinary carpenter. Still, they presented to him their rich gifts of gold, frankincense, and myrrh. These are the first and most famous Christmas presents ever! Do you know why they are so special?

Gold is a gift for a king, that's for sure. In the Bible, gold is used as a symbol for God. And gold doesn't rust. This shows that God is pure and can't be spoiled. The little boy named Jesus was God.

The priests of Israel used frankincense in worship. It is a reminder that Jesus leads our worship to God.

Myrrh is sap from a plant. People find it by cutting through the bark of a tree. This is like Jesus' experience on the cross when a soldier cut him with a spear. Myrrh reminds us that Jesus died for our sins.

These three precious gifts show us just who was living in that little Middle Eastern town of Bethlehem. The wise men did not find just an ordinary baby. They found the King of kings and the very God of the universe!

Dear God, thank you for your Son who was so small, yet the mighty God of Creation!

YOU CAN'T STOP GOD'S PLAN

Herod was furious when he learned that the wise men had outwitted him.
He sent soldiers to kill all the boys in and around Bethlehem
who were two years old and under.
MATTHEW 2:16 NLT

When the wise men spoke to Herod, he sent them to Bethlehem. "Go and search for the child," he told them. "When you have found him, come back and tell me. Then I'll go there and worship him with you." But Herod didn't want to worship Jesus. He was jealous of the baby king and wanted to kill him.

Then one of the wise men had a dream. In it he was warned not to tell Herod where to find Jesus. So the wise men went home by another way. This made Herod angry. He wouldn't be able to find and kill the new king of the Jews. So Herod sent his soldiers to kill every baby boy in Bethlehem!

What happened to Jesus? We know that he wasn't killed. But how did he escape? Joseph, Mary's husband, had a dream. In it God said, "Take the child and his mother. Run away to Egypt and stay there until I tell you to leave. Herod is searching for the child and wants to kill him."

So Joseph did this, and Jesus was saved from death. This story shows that all of the world's power cannot stop God's plan.

Dear God, thank you for protecting Jesus from the evil King Herod.

A NORMAL FAMILY

After the Feast was over, while his parents were returning home,
the boy Jesus stayed behind in Jerusalem,
but they were unaware of it.
LUKE 2:43 NIV

When Jesus was twelve years old, he went with his family to Jerusalem. There was a festival going on called Passover. He and his family probably walked all the way there with others from Nazareth.

The festival ended, and the people from Nazareth began their journey home. Mary and Joseph didn't realize that Jesus wasn't with them because there was such a crowd of friends and relatives walking together. Children were running around, donkeys and camels were braying. At the end of the day, they looked for Jesus. He wasn't there! They must have been surprised and worried.

Have you ever been lost, even for just a few minutes? This happens a lot. It's no one's fault. Mom and Dad look one way and their child goes the other.

Mary and Joseph hurried to Jerusalem to look for Jesus. It took a whole day to get back there. It took them several more days to find Jesus.

This tells us that Jesus lived in a normal family. Yes, he was God. But Jesus and his mother, Joseph and his children were common—just like everyone else. Even the boy Jesus could get lost from his parents!

Dear God, thank you for sending Jesus to be a normal kid like me.

RESPECT FOR PARENTS

After three days they found him in the temple courts,
sitting among the teachers, listening to them and asking them questions.
LUKE 2:46 NIV

What was Jesus doing in Jerusalem? Was he sitting in the dust somewhere crying because he was lost? No, he wasn't afraid. There were no tears in his eyes. He wasn't even worried. It seemed he didn't know his parents were gone. Jesus was busy with the teachers at the temple. He was listening to them and asking them questions.

Remember, he was just a twelve-year-old boy. There he was

among aged, bearded, religious men. The other people in the temple were amazed because Jesus had so much wisdom. No wonder! Jesus was God.

When his parents found him, they asked, "Why have you treated us like this?" But Jesus didn't know he had done anything wrong. He'd been busy talking with the teachers. So he was surprised that he had caused his parents to worry. He was just taking care of his Father's business. Jesus was in his Father's house, the temple, talking about godly things.

Even though Jesus' Father was God, Jesus obeyed his earthly parents. He didn't put up a fuss or complain when he went with Mary and Joseph back to Nazareth. He was a respectful son.

Dear God, help me to respect my parents just like Jesus did.

JOHN THE BAPTIST

In those days John the Baptist came,
preaching in the Desert of Judea and saying,
"Repent, for the kingdom of heaven is near."
MATTHEW 3:1–2 NIV

John was Jesus' cousin. His job in God's plan was to preach to the Jews before Jesus came. John told them, "Turn away from your sins and turn to God. The kingdom of heaven is near."

Jesus came to bring the kingdom of heaven to the earth. John introduced Jesus to Israel and hoped the Jews would believe in him. But Israel didn't want Jesus to be their king. They rejected him.

God didn't give up on Israel, though. He sent men and women who had followed Jesus and learned from him to Israel, too. They also told the Jews, "God's kingdom has come." Their story is told in the Bible in the book of Acts.

Sadly, Israel still didn't listen. So God has set the Jews aside for a little while. Those of us who are not Jews now have a chance to know Jesus. What a joy this is!

This doesn't mean that the Jews won't finally get God's kingdom. That will happen in the end, when Jesus comes back for them. Then they'll repent just as John asked them to do so long ago. Then, God will give them the promised kingdom.

Dear God, thank you for giving me a chance to know Jesus!

A LAMB FOR SACRIFICE

The next day John saw Jesus coming toward him and said,
"Look! There is the Lamb of God who takes away the sin of the world!"
JOHN 1:29 NLT

Everyone knows that Jesus wasn't really a lamb. He was a man. For his whole life, he wasn't like a lamb at all. He was strong and bold until the end. Then he became like a lamb. The Bible says that when Jesus died, "He was led as a lamb to the slaughter. And as a sheep is silent before the shearers, he did not open his mouth."

In the times of the Old Testament, people made sacrifices to God for their sins. These sacrifices were usually lambs. Year after year, people made these sacrifices. Then Jesus came. He was the last sacrifice for sin. No one has to kill a little lamb again because of sin. Jesus is the Lamb of God whose death took away the sin of the world. "For God so loved the world that he gave his only Son, so that everyone who believes in him will not perish but have eternal life."

Dear God, thank you for giving Jesus to be the sacrifice for my sin.

BAPTISM

Then Jesus came from Galilee to the Jordan to be baptized by John.

MATTHEW 3:13 NIV

Jesus lived in Galilee. This was in the far north of Israel. He traveled from there all the way to the Jordan River to be baptized. But John didn't want to baptize Jesus. John knew Jesus was the new king of the Jews.

John said to Jesus, "You should baptize me. Why are you coming to me for baptism?"

John was no better than anyone else. Yes, he told Israel that they needed Jesus, but he knew he needed Jesus, too. Still, Jesus wanted John to baptize him. Why?

Jesus preached the same thing John did: "Repent, the kingdom of heaven is here." But Jesus didn't just talk. He also lived in the way he hoped others would live.

Have you ever heard someone say, "Actions speak louder than words"? Well, Jesus knew this was true. So he did what he expected others to do. He was baptized for the kingdom.

Dear God, help me to live like Jesus lived.

THE BREAD OF LIFE

Then the Devil came and said to him,
"If you are the Son of God, change these stones into loaves of bread."
But Jesus told him, "No! The Scriptures say,
'People need more than bread for their life;
they must feed on every word of God.'"

MATTHEW 4:3–4 NLT

Two things we cannot live without are food and water. Even Jesus got hungry. But he knew that people needed two kinds of food. There is food for the body and food for the soul. Everyone knows about the food for our body. Jesus came to teach us about the other food. In fact, it was one of the first things he talked about. "People need more than bread for their life," Jesus said. "They must feed on every word of God."

One day Jesus was out in the countryside. Thousands of people came there to see and hear him. When it came time to eat, no one had any food. With five loaves of bread and two fish, Jesus fed them all. The same people crowded around Jesus the next day. He told them, "You only came here because I fed you yesterday. But God gives you the true bread from heaven."

"Please, give us this bread," they begged.

Jesus answered them, "I am the bread of life. Come to me and you will never be hungry."

No one can go without food. No one should go without knowing that Jesus is the real food.

Dear God, help me to remember that Jesus is the real Bread of Life.

DANGEROUS THINGS

Then the Devil took him to Jerusalem, to the highest point of the Temple,
and said, "If you are the Son of God, jump off!"
MATTHEW 4:5–6 NLT

Did anyone ever say to you, "I dare you"? This is what the devil was saying to Jesus in these verses: "I dare you to jump off of the wall of the temple. After all, didn't God promise that the angels would protect you?"

But Jesus wouldn't do it.

The Bible promises that God will protect you. But this doesn't mean that you can do dangerous things just for fun. If you play in the street, a car might hit you. If you play with matches, you might get burnt. The world is a dangerous place. The way to not get hurt is to be careful. To be careful means you care about yourself and others. So don't look for danger, and don't play with danger.

Sometimes danger comes to you without your looking for it. Someone you love may get deathly sick. Or you may get separated from your parents and be lost for a short time. If you are in danger, call on God for help. But don't tempt God by looking for danger or accepting a dare.

Dear God, please protect me and help me to stay away from danger.

THE LIGHT

"The people living in darkness have seen a great light;
on those living in the land of the shadow of death a light has dawned."
MATTHEW 4:16 NIV

Look around you. What do you see? There is the room you're sitting in as you read this book. You see the walls, floor, and ceiling. Maybe there is furniture, a rug on the floor, and pictures on the wall. All these things have shapes and colors that you see through your eyes. But without light, you would see nothing.

Imagine there were no light in your room. What would you see? Nothing! You would not even see the words on this page. Now imagine that your world had never had any light. Would you know the color of the rug? No. Would you know the true shape of a chair or lamp? No. You wouldn't even know your own face because you couldn't see it in a mirror.

The Bible says that when Jesus walked in Galilee he was a great light. Yes, there was sunshine in Galilee. There were lamps and fires for light. But the people were sitting in darkness. Their darkness was in their minds. They could not understand anything about God. When Jesus came, he was the light showing God to the people of Galilee.

The same is true today. Without Jesus, people cannot understand God.

Dear God, thank you for sending Jesus to light the way to you.

SEEING JESUS

"Come, follow me," Jesus said, "and I will make you fishers of men."
At once they left their nets and followed him.
MATTHEW 4:19—20 NIV

Jesus, the great light, was walking along the beach and some fishermen were there. Two were in their boat on the sea fishing with nets. Two others were near their boat on the shore. They were mending their nets with their father. Then these men, whose names were Peter, Andrew, James, and John, saw Jesus. He called to them, and they left everything to follow him.

Peter, Andrew, James, and John were just like everyone else in Galilee. They were sitting in darkness. Think of your dark room again. Can you move around a room where there is no light? No. Not without danger of hurting yourself or breaking something. All you can really do is sit there. You can't go anywhere. The people in Galilee were going nowhere because they had no light to see God. But when Jesus, the great light, called the fishermen, they didn't wait. Immediately they could see enough to follow Jesus.

All this happened about two thousand years ago. But the same is true today. People don't move or change until they see Jesus. Because he is the light, they can see themselves. They can also see the world around them as it really is.

Dear God, thank you for Jesus and his light in our lives.

YOUR BEST FRIEND

As Jesus went on from there,
he saw a man named Matthew sitting at the tax collector's booth.
"Follow me," he told him, and Matthew got up and followed him.

MATTHEW 9:9 NIV

Jesus lived in the land of Israel. In those days, another nation ruled Israel. This nation was Rome. The Romans forced the people of Israel to pay taxes to them. This was not fair, but they made them do it because they had the power.

Matthew, the man who wrote the gospel of Matthew, was an Israelite. But he worked for the Romans. He collected taxes from his own people and gave the money to Rome. The people of Israel hated

men like Matthew because tax collectors were dishonest, and they worked for Israel's enemy. So Matthew was despised and rejected.

Jesus knew how this felt. He loved his people, and he told them about God. He didn't collect taxes from them; instead, he loved them. He healed them and fed them. But some people in Israel hated him, especially the leaders.

Jesus loved Matthew the tax collector just as he loved everyone. He called to Matthew, "Come and follow me." So Matthew left everything and followed the Lord.

Sometimes you may feel like Matthew—that you have no friends or that people hate you. But remember, you do have a friend—Jesus. He knows all about you, and he loves you all the time.

Dear God, thank you for always being my best friend.

THE GREAT PHYSICIAN

When the Pharisees saw this, they asked his disciples,
"Why does your teacher eat with tax collectors and 'sinners'?"
On hearing this, Jesus said, "It is not the healthy who need a doctor, but the sick."
MATTHEW 9:11–12 NIV

When I was a boy, I knew some kids who always seemed to be getting hurt. They always had stitches, a broken arm, or a black eye. Maybe you're not like them. But you've probably been to the doctor with an ear infection or a sore throat. Everybody has doctor's checkups, but usually we only visit the doctor when we're sick. Why? Because when we're well, we don't need the doctor.

Jesus liked to sit down to dinner at his friends' houses. Other people would have dinner with him there, too. They wanted to be with him because they knew they needed him. Some of the people at the dinner were publicans. They were tax collectors, like Matthew, who were hated in Israel. Other people at dinner with Jesus were sinners. The religious leaders of Israel hated them. But Jesus loved them all. They went to see Jesus because they knew they were sick with sin. He was their doctor, and he healed them. He healed their bodies, their souls, and their spirits.

Dear God, thank you for sending Jesus to save sinners like me.

SICK PEOPLE

When he heard this, Jesus replied,
"Healthy people don't need a doctor—sick people do."
MATTHEW 9:12 NLT

The strict religious teachers in Jesus' day were the Pharisees. They always had people following Jesus around, hoping to catch him in a mistake. They were there when Jesus was eating with tax collectors and sinners.

Now the Pharisees thought they had him. They could use this to prove that Jesus wasn't a good man. "After all," they could say, "he eats with the wrong people." So they asked the disciples, "Why is Jesus eating with such outcasts?"

Jesus answered them, "People who are sick need a doctor."

Those sinners and tax collectors knew they needed the Lord. They needed his forgiveness and love. The Pharisees were just as needy but they didn't know it. They were sick with sin like everyone else and needed Jesus to heal them. But they thought they were better than other people. They thought they were always right and that their religion made them holy.

They didn't understand that every human being is sick with sin. Sin is like a cancer that no one can cure—no one but Jesus. He came to cure all of humanity. This was done when Jesus died on the cross. His death took away sin and healed us all.

Dear God, thank you for Jesus, who healed me from my sin.

MEN AND WOMEN

*After this, Jesus traveled about from one town and village to another,
proclaiming the good news of the kingdom of God.
The Twelve were with him, and also some women.*

LUKE 8:1–2 NIV

Do you know the names of the Lord's disciples? They are Simon (whom Jesus named Peter); Andrew (Simon's brother), the brothers James and John, Philip and Bartholomew, Matthew and Thomas, another James, Simon the Zealot, Judas, and Judas Iscariot, who betrayed Jesus.

You can see that these are all men. In the days of Jesus, men controlled almost everything. Women had no power. Jesus changed this. Many women followed Jesus and did important things. Mary Magdalene, Mary the mother of James, and Salome were the first to discover Jesus' resurrection. Joanna was the wife of a powerful government officer. She and Susanna not only followed Jesus, but also gave him money. Mary of Bethany and her sister, Martha, often gave Jesus hospitality. Their home was a comfort to him.

The Bible says only one of Jesus' disciples watched as he died. That was John. But at least three women were there—Mary, Jesus' mother; another woman named Mary; and Mary Magdalene. Later, other women would become important in the church. These are women like Lydia, Priscilla, and Junia. Since those days, women have always been important in the church.

Dear God, thank you for loving all men and women.

GOD THE FATHER

"O righteous Father, the world doesn't know you,
but I do; and these disciples know you sent me.
And I have revealed you to them and will keep on revealing you.
I will do this so that your love for me may be in them and I in them."

JOHN 17:25–26 NLT

My father and I shared the same name—Daniel. His friends called him Dan. Only my sisters and I could call him Dad. We were his children. We were born of him.

My dad has passed away, but I remember him well. I know a lot about his life. But he doesn't just live in my memories. Much more, he lives deep within me. I'm not exactly like him, but he gave me physical life. His life is in me. I look a little like him and act like him sometimes. This is because he is my father.

It is the same with God. People who are born of God call him Father. Jesus told us that this is God's name.

My physical father is Dan Partner. In many ways, I'm just like him. My spiritual father is God. My spirit is born of God's Spirit. God's life is in me. Deep inside, I am like my Father God. This is hard to understand. The first person to hear of this was named Nicodemus. He was educated and wise. He heard about being born of God. All he could say was, "How can these things be?" We've been given the Bible to help us understand this wonder.

Dear God, thank you being our Father, and thank you for the Bible to help us understand you.

MiRACLES

Jesus told the servants, "Fill the jars with water."
When the jars had been filled to the brim, he said,
"Dip some out and take it to the master of ceremonies."
JOHN 2:7–8 NLT

One day, Jesus' mother was a guest at a wedding celebration in a village called Cana. Jesus and his followers were there, too. But the wine ran out before the feast was over. Jesus' mother told him, "They have no more wine." And she said to the servants, "Do whatever he tells you."

Six stone water pots were there. They were used for Jewish religious ceremonies and held twenty to thirty gallons each. Jesus told the servants, "Fill the jars with water." They filled the jars to the brim.

Then Jesus said, "Dip some out and take it to the man in charge of the feast." The man tasted what he thought was water, but Jesus had turned it to wine!

This was the first miracle Jesus ever did. Why do you think Jesus did this miracle? It was a sign showing who Jesus is. Jesus did miracles like these to show his glory and power and to help people believe in him.

Dear God, thank you for miracles that show me your power.

Born Again

Jesus replied, "I assure you, unless you are born again,
you can never see the Kingdom of God."
"What do you mean?" exclaimed Nicodemus.
John 3:3–4 NLT

When you have a question, don't you think your teacher should have the answer? Nicodemus was a teacher for all of Israel. But when Jesus said, "You have to be born again," Nicodemus didn't know what this meant. Jesus told him that it is difficult to explain. It is like trying to follow the wind. We can hear and feel the wind, but we don't know where it came from or where it is going.

By believing in Jesus, a person has a second birth. This is sometimes called the new birth. When it happens, that person is born again. To see this new birth in a person's life, you must look carefully. It's like the wind—very hard to see.

Have you ever seen fruit hanging from a tree? Sometimes it is hard to see because the leaves hide it. A person who is born again has special fruit in his or her life. Look carefully and you may see love, joy, peace, patience, kindness, goodness, faithfulness, gentleness, and self-control. That is how you know if a person has been born again.

Dear God, I want to please you—help me to grow all of your good fruit in my life.

GOD AND SANTA CLAUS

"For God so loved the world that he gave his one and only Son,
that whoever believes in him shall not perish but have eternal life.
For God did not send his Son into the world to condemn the world,
but to save the world through him."

JOHN 3:16–17 NIV

I don't remember ever writing to Santa Claus. I think I just told my parents about the gifts I hoped to receive at Christmas. One Christmas morning I found an army of tiny plastic soldiers carefully set for battle. This was exactly what I'd asked for. I also got my first book that Christmas. It was the one I'd asked for—*The Adventures of Robin Hood.*

This makes me think about prayer. People pray to tell God what they want from him. These are usually blessings like health, safety, and friendship. It is good to pray, but let's remember that God is not Santa Claus. It is important to know that God already gave us the greatest gift. "God so loved the world that he gave his one and only Son." His son is Jesus Christ. He is God's blessing to the whole world.

There is a prayer that God loves to answer. Ask that Christ would dwell in your heart by faith. Pray that you will know the love of Christ and be filled with God. These prayers are recommended in the Bible. God will answer them.

Dear God, thank you for your greatest gift—Jesus Christ.

OUTCASTS

Jesus, tired from the long walk, sat wearily beside the well about noontime.
Soon a Samaritan woman came to draw water, and Jesus said to her,
"Please give me a drink."
JOHN 4:6–7 NLT

It was about noon one day, and Jesus was alone, resting by a well. A woman came to the well to draw out some water. Jesus asked her to give him some. In those days, this wasn't done. Men and women  had nothing to do with each other unless they were married. Plus, the woman in this story was a Samaritan. Jesus was a Jew. The Jews thought they were much better than the Samaritans, and so they never spoke to each other.

Most women in those days got their water in the morning. Then they had what they needed for that day. Plus, they didn't have to carry water in the heat of the day. But this woman was an outcast in her village. She had been married several times. The other women stayed away from her because she was a sinner.

You might say this woman had three strikes against her. She was a sinner. She was a Samaritan. She was a woman. To everyone else, she was out, but not to Jesus. This story shows that Jesus came for the outcasts of this world. He came for sinners and poor people. He came for everyone, no matter who they are.

Dear God, thank you for not playing favorites—you care for everyone.

TOUCHING JESUS

She said to herself, "If I only touch his cloak, I will be healed."
Jesus turned and saw her. "Take heart, daughter," he said,
"your faith has healed you."
And the woman was healed from that moment.
MATTHEW 9:21—22 NIV

Jesus was walking through a crowd of people. They all wanted to see him, as if he was a movie star. In the crowd was a woman who was quite sick. She'd been bleeding and slowly dying for twelve years. She'd been to many doctors but none of them could heal her or even help her. All her money was gone from paying them. So the woman was not only sick, she was also penniless.

This poor woman must have heard about Jesus' miracles. She wanted to be healed, too. The doctors couldn't heal her, but she believed Jesus could. "If I just touch the hem of his garment," she thought, "I'll be healed." So as the crowd pushed and shoved around her, she touched Jesus' robe. Even in the hubbub, Jesus knew one person had touched him. The bleeding woman had touched him in faith, and healing power had gone out of him.

Today there is still a crowd pushing and shoving around Jesus. People want to be known as Christians. They want to be seen with the Lord. But Jesus would rather we be like that woman who quietly touched him in faith.

Dear God, help me to have great faith in you.

LOOK TO JESUS

About three o'clock in the morning Jesus came to them, walking on the water.
MATTHEW 14:25 NLT

Jesus' followers were once taught a lesson on how to trust the Lord.

One day, Jesus was alone on a mountain praying. Some of his followers were in a boat, rowing across a huge lake. Nighttime came, and the boat was far away from land. They were having trouble rowing because of strong winds.

Jesus came to help them late at night. He was walking on the water! The disciples saw him and screamed. They thought Jesus was a ghost.

Jesus said, "It's all right. I'm here! Don't be afraid."

Peter, one of the men in the boat, called out, "Lord, if it's you, tell me to come to you by walking on water."

"Come on," Jesus said.

Peter went over the side of the boat and walked on the water toward Jesus! But then he looked around at the high waves and was terrified. As soon as Peter took his eyes off Jesus, he began to sink. He shouted, "Save me, Lord!"

Jesus reached out and grabbed Peter. "You don't have much faith," Jesus said. "Why did you doubt me?" They climbed back into the boat, and the wind stopped.

Peter lost faith for a simple reason. Instead of looking at Jesus, he looked at the waves. We must never stop looking to Jesus, or we might sink, too!

Dear God, help me to keep my eyes on you and your son, Jesus Christ.

SPEAK FOR YOURSELF

On their arrival in Capernaum, the tax collectors for the Temple tax
came to Peter and asked him, "Doesn't your teacher pay the Temple tax?"
MATTHEW 17:24 NLT

When I was a boy, I didn't try to get in trouble. But sometimes I just made mistakes and found myself in trouble. Once, I was playing with a ball in the house—a real mistake. In the living room of my dad's house was a big window. You could look out and see all the Rocky Mountains in the West. My ball went through that window and broke it.

One day, Jesus' follower, Peter, made a mistake. He was asked if Jesus paid taxes to the temple. Peter should have said, "I don't know. I'll go and ask him." Instead, without thinking he spoke for Jesus, "Yes he does."

When Peter got home, Jesus asked him about this temple tax. The temple was the place to worship God, and Jesus was God's Son. Why would he have to give money to the temple? Peter understood what Jesus was talking about. He knew he'd made a mistake.

But where would he get the money? Jesus told Peter to go fishing. He would catch a fish, open its mouth, and there find a coin. Peter used this to pay the temple tax. Jesus took care of Peter's mistake and Peter learned this lesson: Don't speak for others.

Dear God, help me to learn to speak only for myself.

THE GREATEST IN THE KINGDOM

At that time the disciples came to Jesus and asked,
"Who is the greatest in the kingdom of heaven?"
MATTHEW 18:1 NIV

Jesus' disciples once asked him, "Who is the greatest in the kingdom of heaven?" You'll be happy to know how Jesus answered. He brought a little child to the disciples and explained that they needed to change and become like that child. Then they could enter the kingdom of heaven.

Why did the disciples need to change? It was because they had asked the wrong question. They wanted to know who was the greatest. They wanted people to think they were the most important of all men. But little children aren't worried about being better or stronger than everyone else. They don't need to because they trust their parents to take care of them. Their parents are the greatest. So they have everything they need.

This is what it means to live in a kingdom. No one is greater than the king. You depend on him and trust in him. Everything you have and all you are comes from him. Adults must have the same trust in God. They must see that only God is the greatest in the kingdom.

Dear God, help me to remember that you are the greatest.

HUNGRY PEOPLE

Then he told the people to sit down on the grass.
And he took the five loaves and two fish, looked up toward heaven,
and asked God's blessing on the food. Breaking the loaves into pieces, he gave some
of the bread and fish to each disciple, and the disciples gave them to the people.
MATTHEW 14:19 NLT

In this story, Jesus and his disciples traveled far away from any city. Thousands of men, women, and children followed them. In fact, there were five thousand men, plus the women and children. They listened to Jesus speak all day and watched him heal the sick. Soon, the day was over. It was late, and the huge crowd was hungry. Their stomachs were growling, and the children were cranky and tired.

The disciples wanted to send the people away to find food. They didn't show much care for the hungry people. But the Lord loved them. They didn't have to leave to find food. Jesus told the disciples to feed them. The poor disciples must have thought, *He's crazy! How can we feed thousands of people?* Five loaves of bread and two fish were all they had.

"Bring them to me," said Jesus. Then he told the people to sit down on the grass. He took the bread and fish and looked up to heaven. Jesus prayed for God's blessing on the food. Then he broke the loaves of bread into pieces. The disciples gave it to the crowd, and many thousands were fed. This miracle shows that when Jesus comes back, no one will ever again go hungry.

Dear God, thank you for providing for those who are hungry.

FEEDING BODY AND SOUL

Then Jesus took the loaves, gave thanks to God, and passed them out to the people.
Afterward he did the same with the fish. And they all ate until they were full.
John 6:11 NLT

Huge crowds sometimes followed Jesus wherever he went. They'd seen his miracles, and they wanted to see more.

On a warm springtime day, Jesus went up into the hills and sat down. His disciples sat around him. Soon a crowd of people climbed the hill, looking for him. He asked one of his disciples, "Philip, can we buy bread to feed these people?"

Philip replied, "It would take a small fortune to feed them!"

Then Andrew spoke up. "There's a boy here with five loaves of bread and two fish. But what good is that with this huge crowd?"

"Tell everyone to sit down," Jesus ordered. The crowd sat down on the grassy slope. There were five thousand men and even more women and children. Then Jesus took the loaves, gave thanks to God, and passed them out. Afterward he did the same with the fish. And they all ate until they were full.

"Gather the leftovers," Jesus said, "so that nothing is wasted." Twelve baskets were filled with leftovers!

This miracle caused many people to believe in Jesus. It was a sign to help people understand that Jesus is the bread of life. He came not to feed our body, but to feed our soul.

Dear God, thank you for feeding not only my body, but my soul, too.

MIRACLES LEFT OVER

They all ate as much as they wanted,
and they picked up twelve baskets of leftovers.
About five thousand men had eaten from those five loaves,
in addition to all the women and children!
MATTHEW 14:20–21 NLT

How could five loaves of bread feed over five thousand people? I don't know. No one knows. This is a wonderful miracle. God does not want his people to go hungry. He is the Creator. He created the world and everything in it. Surely he can create some pieces of bread in a basket.

The crowds of people ate enough and were filled. But something else about this miracle is even more amazing. There were twelve baskets full of bread and fish left over! When God does a miracle, there are miracles left over.

There were twelve tribes in the nation of Israel. Here there were twelve baskets full of bread. This points forward to the time when God's kingdom has come. At that time, God's blessings will flow to all the nations in the world. God will pour all this out through Israel. The twelve baskets of bread and fish show us Israel in the future. In the kingdom, Israel will hold all of God's blessings for the nations.

Dear God, thank you for your miracles that teach us about your kingdom.

CALL ON THE NAME OF THE LORD

And Jesus answered, "Why are you afraid? You have so little faith!"
Then he stood up and rebuked the wind and waves, and suddenly all was calm.
MATTHEW 8:26 NLT

Do you know how to swim? Some of Jesus' followers didn't. One time when they were in a boat on a big lake, the wind began to tip the boat. It was filling with water! They were afraid even though

Jesus was in the same boat. He wasn't afraid of the storm. In fact, he was asleep! His followers were afraid because they believed more in the storm than in Jesus. So Jesus scolded them: "You have so little faith!" They believed in the wrong thing.

Many people today believe in the wrong thing. They have little faith in Jesus and great faith in the world. Hard times can come to us in this world. They are like the storm in this story. Jesus may seem to be sleeping through your storm, but you should always believe in him. Maybe the storm has come to help you believe in him even more.

Jesus' followers cried out, "Lord, save us!" They did just the right thing. The Bible says, "Anyone who calls on the name of the Lord will be saved."

Dear God, thank you for saving us when we have faith in you.

GOD'S TEACHINGS

Jesus answered, "My teaching is not my own. It comes from him who sent me. If anyone chooses to do God's will, he will find out whether my teaching comes from God or whether I speak on my own."

JOHN 7:16–17 NIV

Jesus lived in a part of Israel called Galilee. This was far away from Jerusalem where the religious leaders lived. These leaders didn't like Jesus and wanted to arrest and kill him.

Jesus once secretly went to a festival in Jerusalem. The religious leaders tried to find him there, asking if anyone had seen him. There was a lot of quiet talk about him in the crowds. Some said, "He's a wonderful man." Others said, "He's nothing but a fake. He tricks people." But no one was brave enough to speak up and say good things about him. Everyone was afraid of getting in trouble with the religious leaders.

Then, in the middle of the festival, Jesus went to the temple. There he began to teach. The religious leaders were surprised. "How does he know so much?" they asked. "He hasn't studied everything we've studied."

Jesus told them, "These are not my own ideas. God sent me and these are God's teachings." He was different from all other teachers, then or now. Anyone who wants to know God can tell that Jesus was teaching God's ideas. He was good and honest, and he only honored God.

Dear God, thank you for sending Jesus to teach us about you.

FOR GOD'S GLORY

So the crowd was divided in their opinion about him.
And some wanted him arrested, but no one touched him.
JOHN 7:43–44 NLT

The religious leaders sent guards to arrest Jesus. They found him on the last day of the festival, the most exciting day of all. The guards saw Jesus shouting to the crowds, "If you are thirsty, come to me! If you believe in me, come and drink! The Bible proclaims that rivers of living water will flow out from inside of you." (When he said, "living water," he meant the Holy Spirit. The Holy Spirit is given to everyone who believes in Jesus.)

When the crowds heard this, some said, "This man is the Prophet."

Others said, "He is the Messiah."

Others argued, "He can't be! Will the Messiah come from Galilee?"

The crowd couldn't agree about him. Some of them even wanted Jesus arrested, but no one touched him.

The guards who had been sent to arrest Jesus went back to the religious leaders. "Why didn't you bring him with you?" they demanded.

The guards could only shrug and say, "We've never heard anyone talk like him!" They knew Jesus talked about God in a different way than the religious leaders. He only wanted God's glory. The leaders wanted glory for themselves. This is why they wanted to kill him.

Dear God, help me to do everything for your glory, just like Jesus did.

JUDGING OTHERS

They made her stand before the group and said to Jesus,
"Teacher, this woman was caught in the act of adultery.
In the Law Moses commanded us to stone such women.
Now what do you say?"
JOHN 8:3–5 NIV

The religious leaders always tried to trick Jesus into doing something wrong so that they could arrest him.

Early one morning, Jesus was in the temple. All kinds of people came to see him, and he sat down and taught them. Just then, the religious leaders came in dragging a woman with them. They showed off the sad woman in front of the crowd.

"Teacher," they said, "this woman was caught sinning. Our law says to stone her to death. What do you say?" They were trying to trap Jesus. They hoped he would say something wrong so they could get him in trouble.

Instead of answering, Jesus stooped down and wrote in the dust with his finger. No one knows what he wrote. Still they demanded an answer, so he stood up and said, "Okay, go ahead and stone her. But only those of you who have never sinned can throw the first stones."

They heard this, and one by one they quietly left the Temple. Only Jesus was left in the middle of the crowd with the woman.

Jesus had shown them that everyone is a sinner. They understood that only God could judge a person's sin.

Dear God, help me not to judge others.

COMFORT IN SADNESS

"Blessed are those who mourn, for they will be comforted."
MATTHEW 5:4 NIV

Once, when I was a boy, I was traveling with my family. We were driving through Kansas on the way to my cousins' house. I remember it was a sunny day in June. All around us were golden fields of wheat. A few trees grew here and there between the fields. I was in the back seat, sitting up so I could see out the windshield to the road ahead. Suddenly, I saw a sparrow. It flew in front of my dad's car and hit the windshield.

I quickly turned and looked out the back window. I wanted to see what had happened to the bird. There it was, rising up high in the blue sky. I thought, *Maybe the sparrow's all right. It's flying away.* But just as fast as it had flown so high, it fell to the earth. I saw it hit the highway behind the car—dead. I sat back on the big seat of that old Chevy. Silently, I sat there, so sad about the sparrow's death. I mourned it until the trip was over.

You have probably felt sadness like this. But just remember at times like these, God promises to comfort you.

Dear God, thank you for promising to comfort me when I am sad.

WHO IS RIGHT?

"Blessed are those who hunger and thirst for righteousness,
for they will be filled."
MATTHEW 5:6 NIV

When I was a boy, we played baseball. Not baseball like you see on television, though, and not like the game you may play in Little League. We'd play this game on a summer afternoon in the lot behind the school. This was a sand lot. It had no grass, just sand and dust. And it was dry, like Colorado always is that time of year.

There were no adults anywhere nearby. We had a bat and ball and each boy had his glove. We'd choose teams of four or five players each and begin to play. But sooner or later, the game would fall apart. There was usually some clash about fair play because someone thought the rules had been broken. But the rules of sandlot baseball are simple. You wouldn't think there would be any argument about them. Still, we fought over them. Each side thought they were right. Those baseball games weren't important. But today, we still all want to be right.

Here's the secret about being right: Only God is always right. So believe in him and you'll be filled with righteousness.

Dear God, help me remember that only you are always right.

SHOWING MERCY

"Blessed are the merciful, for they will be shown mercy."
MATTHEW 5:7 NIV

What is mercy? It's when you see a spider walking across the floor and you don't kill it. You have power over the spider. You may hate the spider. It may give you the creeps. You may be deathly afraid of spiders, afraid that they may bite you or even kill you. But in your mercy, you don't kill the spider. Instead, you let it go on to wherever it is going. You let it live. That is mercy.

Mercy is when you don't pick on someone who is different than you. Maybe a girl has a lot of pimples. Maybe a boy doesn't wear nice clothes or doesn't have a good haircut. You see people making fun of them in the hallway at school. But instead of doing the same, you say, "Hi. How are you?" You treat them kindly, like you treat everyone else. That is mercy.

If you treat others with mercy, it means that you know what mercy is. God treats everyone with mercy. When you know mercy, you know God. And when you show mercy, God will show mercy to you.

Dear God, help me to show mercy to others and receive mercy from you.

PURE IN HEART

"Blessed are the pure in heart, for they will see God."
MATTHEW 5:8 NIV

There was a man named Paul who knew more about God than anyone who has ever lived. Paul wrote half of the books in the New Testament. But before he came to know God, Paul hated Christians and even killed them.

One day he saw the Lord as he was traveling. A bright light shone all around him.

Paul asked, "Who are you, Lord?"

"I am Jesus," was the reply.

The light was so bright that afterwards, Paul couldn't see. God then told Paul to tell people everywhere what he'd seen and heard. Then Paul was healed from his blindness. For the rest of his life, Paul told people about God and God's plan. He spent his whole life seeking God. He wanted to know the Lord more than anything else.

The verse above says that pure people will see God. When will this happen? Paul said, "Today I see God dimly. I hardly know what I'm looking at. It's like I'm looking in a foggy mirror. But in the end, we will see everything perfectly. All that I know now is lacking. But in the end, I will know everything."

In the end, we Christians will all have pure hearts. Then we'll see God.

Dear God, help me to keep a pure heart so that I can see you.

LiVing in PEACE

"Blessed are the peacemakers,
for they will be called sons of God."
MATTHEW 5:9 NIV

When you make peace, you're blessed. Why are you blessed? Because you will be called a child of God.

You'll be like Jesus, God's Son. He is the Prince of Peace. In God's kingdom of peace, Jesus is the prince. He wants you to do your best to live in peace with everyone.

Soon, God's peaceful kingdom will reign on the earth. There will be no more anger or fighting, no more hate or fear. In this kingdom, even the animals will be at peace with one another. The wolf and the lamb will eat together. The lion will be there, too, living peacefully and eating straw like the ox.

Don't you look forward to the time when God's peace rules the earth? God's peace will be so complete and full that even wild animals will be peaceful. Today when you live at peace with others, you are in God's peaceful kingdom.

Dear God, help me to live in peace with everyone.

THE FLAVOR OF GOD

"You are the salt of the earth. But if the salt loses its saltiness,
how can it be made salty again?
It is no longer good for anything, except to be thrown out
and trampled by men."
MATTHEW 5:13 NIV

Have you ever visited the ocean and swam in the water there? Ocean water is different than the water in lakes and rivers. It's salty. If you get a mouthful of ocean water, it tastes very strange. There's so much salt in it that it tastes nasty! If you tried to swallow it, you'd probably gag and spit out the salty water.

There's so much salt in the ocean that it's even in the breeze. You get salt on your skin if you spend just one day on the beach. When you go to the beach, try an experiment on your drive back home. Lick your arm and see how salty your skin tastes. The ocean is so full of salt that some of it will even stay on your skin!

Salt is full of flavor. Many people sprinkle salt on the food they cook. It brings out its taste. Jesus said that we are the salt of the earth. Like salt, we have a special flavor—the flavor of God. Our saltiness makes life better for everyone because we bring the taste of God to them.

Dear God, help me to bring the flavor of you to everyone around me.

THE LIGHT OF THE WORLD

"You are the light of the world.
A city on a hill cannot be hidden."
MATTHEW 5:14 NIV

God is light and we are his light for the world. What a responsibility!

The sun shines every day, but most people are living in darkness. Why? It is because they don't have God as their light. So we must let our light shine. Then God will be seen and known.

Have you ever sung the song, "This little light of mine, I'm gonna let it shine"? Each of us is like a little light. If we all shine together we'll be a city on a hill, shining in the dark. Such a city cannot be hidden.

I grew up near the city of Denver, Colorado. It is called the "Mile High City" because it is a mile above sea level. One night, our family was traveling back home to the city. I was amazed as we came near Denver. It was beautiful. It was a city full of lights—a city on a hill! Denver was so bright, it made the night full of light.

All of us who believe in Jesus are little lights. Together, we make a city of light for God.

Dear God, help me to shine with others to make a city of light for you.

LOVE YOUR ENEMIES

"But I tell you: Love your enemies and pray for those who persecute you,
that you may be sons of your Father in heaven.
He causes his sun to rise on the evil and the good,
and sends rain on the righteous and the unrighteous."
MATTHEW 5:44–45 NIV

In Jesus' day, most people were farmers whose crops needed the sunshine and rain. Do you think every farmer was a good man? No, they weren't. Some were evil and some were good. Others were in between. Some people were just and some were unjust. It is the same today.

Did God make the sunshine and the rainfall only for good and holy farmers? No, the sunshine and rain falls on every field. God makes the sun to rise on the good and the evil. He sends the rain on the just and the unjust. God's love and care extend to all people.

So today, as God's children, let's live by God's grace. With grace, we can love all people just as God does. Jesus said that we should love those who hate us. This means that we should respect and even give thanks for such people. We should do good things for those who hate us. God also said to pray for those who do bad things to us. Without God's grace, this is impossible. The good news is that God gives us this grace for free.

Dear God, please give me the grace to love everyone just as you do.

SECRET PRAYER

"But when you pray, go away by yourself, shut the door behind you,
and pray to your Father secretly.
Then your Father, who knows all secrets, will reward you."
MATTHEW 6:6 NLT

Does your family pray before eating supper? When you go to bed at night, do you pray with your mother or father? It's good to pray at these times. But I want to tell you of a different kind of prayer—

a secret prayer. God our Father can hear us no matter where or when we pray—even in our secret places.

Do you have a secret place deep in the grasses of a meadow? Maybe it is up in the branches of a big oak tree, nearby a gurgling brook, down in the basement, out in the garage, or up in the attic. I once made a secret place in my father's woodpile.

When you're there all alone, it is a good time to say a little prayer to God. Only God will hear you and give you a reward. But unlike your prayer, this isn't a secret reward. Everyone can see God's gift to you. I wonder if you know what this can be. . . . After you've prayed in your secret place, you'll have a smile on your face! This is your reward. God makes you happy. This gift is not only for you, but also for everyone who sees you.

Dear God, thank you for hearing our prayers no matter where we are.

OUR FATHER

"This is how you should pray:
'Our Father in heaven, hallowed be your name.'"
MATTHEW 6:9 NIV

If you go to church with your parents, you may have heard these words. They are the first sentence of a prayer called the Lord's Prayer. Perhaps you even say this prayer at home with your family. Jesus used it to show his followers how to pray. So it's called the Lord's Prayer. It is a model, a pattern of a way to pray.

Notice the words *Our Father.* They tell us to whom we pray. Did you know that you have two fathers? You can see your earthly father. You may play tag with him. Maybe he reads to you before bed. But your heavenly father is God who cannot be seen. Still, God is doing special things for you every day.

You may go to the grocery store to buy food with your mother and father. Your heavenly Father made that food so you can be healthy and grow strong. He also gives warm sunshine so you can play outside. The wind that blows through your hair was sent by God to cool you. Your father on earth may kiss you when he comes home from work. Your heavenly Father sends the sun and wind to kiss you with heavenly kisses.

Dear God, thank you for my earthly father and thank you for being my heavenly Father.

RESPECT GOD'S NAME

"This is how you should pray:
'Our Father in heaven, hallowed be your name.'"
MATTHEW 6:9 NIV

Do you see the word *hallowed* in the Lord's Prayer? This is a strange word. We never hear it except in this prayer. The dictionary says the word *hallow* means, "to make holy; to keep as sacred." It also means to respect. We respect God's name because he is our heavenly Father.

I remember a day long ago when I was a child, maybe about five years old. I was in my bedroom and was very upset about something. I stood in front of my open closet door and loudly said, "God!" But I didn't say that word in a respectful way. I didn't make God's name holy when I said it.

My mother heard me and came into my room. "Never use God's name like that again," she scolded. "Never use our heavenly Father's name in anger."

I remember her warning even though this happened almost fifty years ago! Now I am grown up, and I love God. It makes me sad when I hear people speak the Father's name without respect. When we say God's name, let's say it with love. Then those who hear us will know that his name is sacred, holy, and hallowed.

Dear God, help me to keep your name holy.

GOD'S KINGDOM

"Your kingdom come, your will be done on earth as it is in heaven."
MATTHEW 6:10 NIV

Do you know any fairy tales? They sometimes tell of a king, a queen, and a kingdom. It's fun to imagine their stone castles with turrets and towers. God's kingdom is so much better than this because it's not a fairy tale. Even though his kingdom is not here yet, it is real. The Bible says that in the very end, Christ will come back. Then he'll give the kingdom to his Father. Then God will be all in all.

The last chapters of the Bible tell of the New Jerusalem. This city will come down out of heaven from God. In it, God will dwell with us and wipe away the tears from our eyes. It is a kingdom where there is no more death, sorrow, crying, or pain. This is hard to imagine because today we are sometimes sad. When you fall down and skin your knee, there's pain. But when God is all in all, can there be sadness? When God is all in all, can there be crying? When God is all in all, can there be pain? No.

I'm so glad that Christ is coming with God's kingdom! Aren't you?

Dear God, help me to remember that you will come back soon and take me to your perfect kingdom.

FOOD EVERY DAY

"Give us today our daily bread."
MATTHEW 6:11 NIV

Most people buy their bread from the grocery store. Still, God gives us everything to make bread. God gives the flour, the water, the salt, and the sugar. Even the rain and sun come from God to make the wheat grow. Farmers still have to plant and harvest the wheat. Also,

someone has to work in the bakery to bake the bread. Someone even has to drive the bread truck to the store. There, someone has to put it on the shelves. Someone else works the cash register when we pay for the bread. God gives the makings for bread and the people to bring the bread to us.

When my daughter visits, she says the prayer before supper. She thanks God for all the different hands that bring food to us. Think about fresh green beans. They went on a long journey to get to you, thanks to God. Someone planted the seeds. Someone else picked the beans. Other people shipped them to your town and unpacked them at the store. But God caused the beans to grow. God made the people who bring them to us. God gives us our daily food.

Dear God, thank you for providing food for us to eat.

FORGIVING LIKE GOD

"Forgive us our debts, as we also have forgiven our debtors."
MATTHEW 6:12 NIV

Here's a Bible story that explains this verse:

A king decided to get payment from people who owed him money. One man owed him millions of dollars, but he couldn't pay. The king ordered that the man, his family, and everything he had be sold. The money would pay what was owed. But the man fell down before the king and begged. "Oh, sir, be patient with me. I'll pay it all." The king pitied him, released him, and forgave his debt.

The man went free. He then found someone who owed him a few thousand dollars. He grabbed him by the throat. "Pay me now," he demanded. This man fell down and begged for more time. "Be patient and I'll pay it." Instead, he was arrested and jailed until he could pay.

People who saw this went to the king and told him what happened. The king spoke to the man. "You're evil! I forgave you millions of dollars. Shouldn't you forgive others, just as I did?" Then the angry king sent the man to prison until he had paid every penny.

So the Bible tells us, "Be kind to each other, tenderhearted, forgiving one another, just as God through Christ has forgiven you."

Dear God, help me to forgive others, just as you have forgiven me.

TRUE TREASURE

"Don't store up treasures here on earth,
where they can be eaten by moths and get rusty,
and where thieves break in and steal.
Store your treasures in heaven."
MATTHEW 6:19–20 NLT

What is your favorite toy? My nine-year-old grandson has two huge containers full of Legos. For his birthday, a friend always gives him another Lego toy. He never seems to get tired of them. He loves building things with Legos. He probably thinks about playing with them even when he's away from home. The Legos are his treasure.

He may not know it, but his mother also played with Legos. When she was a little girl, she had a huge container full of Lego pieces. She spent many evenings building with them. But now she's grown up and enjoys other things.

Red, green, yellow, and blue plastic Legos can be lost or stolen. So can all the treasures that we store up on earth. But God is better than these. Nothing can ruin or replace him. Nothing is more enjoyable than him. Thieves cannot steal him from us. God is our true treasure.

Dear God, thank you for being my greatest treasure.

GOD CARES FOR ALL

"Look at the birds.
They don't need to plant or harvest or put food in barns
because your heavenly Father feeds them.
And you are far more valuable to him than they are."
MATTHEW 6:26 NLT

One morning I woke up to a chorus of crows, but their song is not so beautiful. They call out, "Caw, caw!" I heard one crow loudly "Caw!" four times. Then, "Caw!" five times. Then six. In the distance, I faintly heard another crow answering back "Caw!" four times. Then "Caw!" five times. Then six. They were singing together.

The crows' song is not pretty like those of other songbirds. Still, our heavenly Father feeds them, even though they do not work or put money in the bank.

Every day I walk around a pond in a park near my house. There I see many crows, pigeons, seagulls, ducks, geese, sparrows, and swallows. The heavenly Father feeds them, too. Sometimes they are so full they won't eat the bread I throw to them.

We don't need to worry about what we will eat or drink. The birds tell us this. Since our Father takes care of them, surely he takes care of us, too.

Dear God, thank you for taking care of the birds—and me!

GOD DELIGHTS IN HIS CREATION

*"And if God cares so wonderfully for flowers that are here today
and gone tomorrow, won't he more surely care for you?"*
MATTHEW 6:30 NLT

Think about the rain. It comes down on everything—on roses, poppies, lilies, dandelions, moss, weeds, everything! Why? Because God cares about all these things.

But there are so many things to care about in the universe. Why would God be concerned with flowers? The answer is found in Genesis. It says that when God made the light, "It was good." Then God made the dry land and the seas. "And God saw that it was good." He grew all kinds of plants on the earth. "And God saw that it was good." Next, God made the sun, moon, and stars. What did God think of this? "And God saw that it was good." Then God made fish and birds. "And God saw that it was good." Then all kinds of animals were made. "And God saw that it was good."

Six times in Genesis, God saw that it was good. This means that God enjoys his Creation. It is delightful to him. This is why the rain falls on all things. God cares for it all. Since God sends rain on each and every little flower, you know that he cares for you, too!

Dear God, thank you for caring about me!

VISION PROBLEMS

*"And why worry about a speck in your friend's eye
when you have a log in your own?"*
MATTHEW 7:3 NLT

"You did this!" she says.

"Well, you did that!" you answer angrily. Around and around you go, arguing with your friend. There is no end to it, until your friend sadly goes home. Then you may think, *I'll never play with her again!* But you really don't mean that.

Here's what happened: You couldn't see that you were being mean to your friend. You could only see your friend being mean to you. The Bible says this is like having a log in your eye. Meanwhile, your friend only has a splinter in her eye. This is not a real log. The idea of a log in your eye is God's way of saying, "You can't see your own mistakes."

If you have a log in your eye, how can you see your friend? Take the log out of your eye. Suddenly you can see what a good friend you have. How can you take the log out of your eye? Be kind and don't argue.

If your friend argues with you, don't argue back. Don't be mean to her. Without that log in your eye, you'll see what a good friend you have. You'll be glad she's your friend.

Dear God, help me to see my own mistakes, not the mistakes of others.

KNOCKING IN PRAYER

"Keep on asking, and you will be given what you ask for.
Keep on looking, and you will find. Keep on knocking,
and the door will be opened."
MATTHEW 7:7 NLT

Once there was a little girl in the second grade. Spring vacation came, and someone had to take the class's pet bunny home. The little girl's teacher was going to pick a student for this.

The little girl wanted to bring the bunny home so badly she could feel it! So her mother prayed with her that this would happen. She and her mother knocked on God's door about the bunny. The next day the little girl went to school. Her teacher had decided not to choose a student to take the bunny. Instead, she put all the students' names in a hat and drew one name. That person would take the bunny home for vacation. The mother knew that nothing is too hard for God. Again, she and the girl knocked on God's door asking for the bunny.

Do you know the end of this story? Yes, the teacher drew that little girl's name out of the hat! She got to take the class's bunny home during spring vacation. The girl and her mother knocked, and God opened the door for them.

Dear God, thank you for hearing and answering our prayers.

THE GOLDEN RULE

"Do for others what you would like them to do for you."
MATTHEW 7:12 NLT

This verse is known as the Golden Rule. It says that you should treat others the way you want to be treated. Most people, even those who are not Christians, know this rule. They may not know it that it comes from the Bible, but they know what it says. They also know if we all followed this rule, the world would be a wonderful place.

My wife is a second grade teacher at a public school. Before the school year begins, she makes a special sign. It says, "Do to others what you want them to do to you." These words are written on shiny gold paper and put above her classroom door. On the first day of school, she tells the students that this is their Golden Rule. If they follow this rule, there will be no other rules.

As the year passes, some students listen carefully in class. Others play well with each other. Some do an act of kindness for someone else. These are "Golden Students." Why are they golden? Because they obey the Golden Rule. Like gold, they are precious in the classroom. When you follow the Golden Rule, you become a golden person.

Dear God, help me to treat others the way I want to be treated.

SPIRITUAL FRUIT

"By their fruit you will recognize them."
MATTHEW 7:16 NIV

My wife's grandmother was born in 1900, over a hundred years ago! When she was a little girl, she worked on her family's farm and didn't go to school much. She stopped going to school after the third grade.

Grandma Jones didn't talk about God a lot. But she did read her Bible every night before bed. She even wrote a poem once about her loving heavenly Father. Grandma Jones could cook and crochet better than anybody in town. Her cinnamon rolls were the yummiest I've ever tasted. She had very little money, but she often gave her cinnamon rolls away to her neighbors. She also crocheted hundreds of beautiful potholders and gave them all away.

Grandma Jones was generous and kind, loving and good. She believed in Jesus with her whole heart. But she didn't talk about this. She was like a tree that quietly gives good fruit. The things Grandma Jones did were her fruits. The way she lived her life showed the world that she loved God.

Dear God, help me to show others that I love you by what I do.

ACTIONS SPEAK LOUDLY

"Yes, the way to identify a tree or a person is by the kind of fruit that is produced."
MATTHEW 7:20 NLT

Have you ever heard the saying, "Actions speak louder than words"? This is what these verses are talking about. For example, what if one day someone says, "I love God." But the next day they lie, steal, or cheat? Their actions speak louder than their words. The things they do show that they don't really love God.

The Bible explains this by picturing a fruit tree. A healthy apple tree gives firm, sweet apples that are just the right color. In other words, it brings forth good fruit. An unhealthy tree can't give good apples. Faith in God can make you a healthy tree. Then, your words and your actions will be the same.

A poet once wrote about this:

Oh the joy of those who delight in doing what the Lord wants!
They are like trees planted along the riverbank.
They bear fruit each season without fail.
Their leaves never dry up, and everything they do thrives.
But this is not true of sinful people.
They are worthless to God, and are scattered by the wind.

Dear God, help me to keep my actions and my words pleasing to you.

FOOD AND HOUSES

"Anyone who listens to my teaching and obeys me is wise,
like a person who builds a house on solid rock."
MATTHEW 7:24 NLT

Jesus taught there are two kinds of food. The food for our body is very important. It should be healthy food because it builds our bodies. If we use bad food, our bodies will be unhealthy. Foods with too much sugar and fat can't build a healthy body. But there is also food for our soul. The best food for our soul is Jesus. When we believe in Jesus, He is food to our soul and makes our spirits strong.

We also have two kinds of houses. The houses or apartments we live in give shelter to our bodies. If they aren't built well, we could get cold, wet, or sick. But there is also a spiritual house, which no one sees. This house is built upon what we hear and what we do.

By reading the Bible, we hear the words of Jesus. For example, he said, "Do for others what you would like them to do for you." You can build your life on these words. Jesus said that these words explain all that is taught in the Bible. This is the Golden Rule. If you hear this rule and do it, your spiritual house won't fall.

Dear God, I want to make my spiritual house strong—help me to follow the Golden Rule.

JESUS IS GOD

A man with leprosy came and knelt before him and said,
"Lord, if you are willing, you can make me clean."
Jesus reached out his hand and touched the man.
"I am willing," he said. "Be clean!"
Immediately he was cured of his leprosy.
MATTHEW 8:2–3 NIV

One of the first miracles Jesus did was to heal a man from leprosy. He did this to show who he was and why he lived.

Leprosy is an awful disease of the skin and nervous system. The ancient Jews thought God was unhappy with a person who had leprosy. Several well-known people got the disease because they had sinned. One of these was Moses' sister, Miriam. Another was the king of Judah, Uzziah.

Jesus wanted to show that he had come to take away sin, and so he healed lepers. The people of Jesus' time believed that only God could cure leprosy. After all, they thought leprosy came from God because of sin. The doctors of the day didn't even try to cure it. Jesus proved that he was God by healing many lepers.

A man once asked Jesus, "Are you really the Messiah we've been waiting for, or should we keep looking for someone else?"

Jesus told him, "The blind see, the lame walk, the lepers are cured, the deaf hear, the dead are raised to life, and the Good News is being preached to the poor." His miracles prove that Jesus is God.

Dear God, thank you for your healing power.

JESUS' POWER

Some people brought to him a paralyzed man on a mat.
Seeing their faith, Jesus said to the paralyzed man,
"Take heart, son! Your sins are forgiven."
MATTHEW 9:2 NLT

Here's a man who was paralyzed. All he could do was lie on his bed. One day his friends brought him to Jesus. Jesus saw their faith and told the sick man that his sins were forgiven.

Religious people were watching Jesus that day. They were shocked and mad at him. *Only God can forgive sins!* they thought. In other words, they didn't believe Jesus was God.

Jesus is God. He knew the evil thoughts these people had against him. He asked, "Is it easier to forgive sins or to make this man walk?" Neither is easy to do. In fact, both are impossible for anyone except God. Only God can forgive sins. Only God can make a paralyzed man walk.

Jesus decided to show these religious men that he was God. He had the power to forgive sins. So he did what no human being can do. He told the paralyzed man to pick up his bed and go to his own house. The man was healed!

Still today, people think Jesus was just a great teacher and a good man. They need to read this story. It tells that Jesus is God.

Dear God, thank you for sending Jesus to show us your power.

NO ORDINARY MAN

Then Jesus turned to the paralyzed man and said,
"Stand up, take your mat, and go on home, because you are healed!"
And the man jumped up and went home!
MATTHEW 9:6—7 NLT

Some people in Israel thought Jesus was just an ordinary man, especially the religious leaders. But when Jesus told the paralyzed man to stand and walk, the man did it! He was no longer paralyzed! He stood up and walked home. This proved to everyone that God had healed him.

That man must have been happier than he had ever been in his life. He could finally walk! Many people saw the once-paralyzed man walking. They were amazed and praised and thanked God. They didn't question what the Lord had done. They believed that Jesus was God because they saw that he had the power of God.

Someday you may find people who question your simple faith in God. Even religious leaders can do this. The people who saw Jesus heal the paralyzed man were amazed. They were happy and adored God for what had happened. But the religious leaders thought they were smarter than the regular people. This still happens today. Some Christians look down on people with simple faith. But this doesn't matter. The Lord is God, no matter what people think.

Dear God, help me to show others that Jesus is no ordinary man.

FROM DEATH TO LIFE

When Jesus entered the ruler's house and saw the flute players and the noisy crowd,
he said, "Go away. The girl is not dead but asleep."
But they laughed at him. After the crowd had been put outside,
he went in and took the girl by the hand, and she got up.
MATTHEW 9:23–25 NIV

An important man came to see Jesus one day. He told the Lord that his daughter had just died. He believed that if Jesus would simply touch his daughter, she would live again. So Jesus, with his disciples,

followed the man to his house. When they got there, the house was in a hubbub. The people in the neighborhood had come to comfort the family. Plans were being made for the funeral. Musicians were playing sad music. This stirred up sorrow in the girl's family and friends.

Jesus told all the people to stop the ruckus. "The girl is only sleeping," he said.

The noisemakers thought he was crazy and laughed at him. Finally, the people made room and Jesus went in to see the young girl. He took her hand, and she arose from the bed. She was alive again!

Imagine someone who was dead being made alive! This is the greatest miracle. But the Bible says that everyone who has died will be made alive again. God is so amazing and full of life. He will bring everyone back from death. Then they will all see God.

Dear God, thank you for your power to bring us from death to life.

THE PROBLEM OF SIN

So they went up to the roof, took off some tiles,
and lowered the sick man down into the crowd, still on his mat,
right in front of Jesus. Seeing their faith,
Jesus said to the man, "Son, your sins are forgiven."
LUKE 5:19–20 NLT

One day while Jesus was teaching, some religious leaders were sitting nearby. Such men were always around. They came from every village and from as far away as Jerusalem. Some other men came to where Jesus was teaching, carrying a paralyzed man on a mat. They couldn't push through the crowd to Jesus, so they went up to the roof and opened a hole. They lowered the sick man down into the crowd right in front of Jesus. Jesus said to the man, "Son, your sins are forgiven."

The religious leaders said to each other, "Who does this man think he is? He is mocking God! Only God can forgive sins."

Jesus knew what they were thinking. He asked them, "Is it easier to say, 'Your sins are forgiven' or 'Get up and walk'? I'll prove that I have the power to forgive sins."

Then Jesus said to the paralyzed man, "Stand up. Take your mat, and go on home. You're healed!" Everyone watched as the man jumped up and went home praising God.

Jesus healed many people in his day. But this was not the reason he came. This story plainly shows why God sent Jesus to us. It was to take care of the problem of sin.

Dear God, thank you for sending your son, Jesus, to forgive our sins.

JESUS' LOVING HEART

Then he went up and touched the coffin, and those carrying it stood still. He said,
"Young man, I say to you, get up!" The dead man sat up and began to talk,
and Jesus gave him back to his mother.

LUKE 7:14–15 NIV

Although Jesus was a man, he was also God. This is hard to understand, but it's true. It wasn't hard for him to heal the sick and even bring people back from death. He did these things so that people would know who he was.

Jesus and his followers went to a village called Nain. A huge crowd trailed along with him. As he came to the village gate, a funeral procession was coming out. A boy had died, and he was the only son of a widow. Many villagers mourned with the poor woman. When the Lord saw her, his heart overflowed with love and kindness. "Don't cry!" he said. Then he walked over to the coffin and touched it. The men carrying it stopped. "Young man, get up!" he said. Then the boy who had been dead sat up and began to talk to those around him! Jesus gave him back to his mother.

The crowd praised God. "A mighty prophet has come to us," they cried. But they didn't understand. Jesus didn't mean to show he was a great prophet. He wanted them to see his loving heart. This miracle shows we should care about people's suffering just as Jesus did.

Dear God, help me to love people like you do.

FORGIVEN MUCH

"Two men owed money to a certain moneylender. . . .
Neither of them had the money to pay him back, so he canceled the debts of both.
Now which of them will love him more?" Simon replied, "I suppose the one who
had the bigger debt canceled." "You have judged correctly," Jesus said.

LUKE 7:41–43 NIV

One of the religious leaders of Jesus' time was named Simon. He asked Jesus to come to his home for a meal. So Jesus went there and sat down to eat. An immoral woman heard he was there. She walked in the house weeping. Her tears fell on his feet. She knelt down and dried them with her hair. Then she kissed his feet and put perfume on them.

This offended Simon. He said to himself, "This proves that Jesus isn't God's prophet. If he were, he'd know what kind of woman is touching him. She's a sinner!"

Jesus knew what Simon was thinking. "When I came here," he said, "you didn't give me water to wash my feet. She has washed them with her tears. You didn't give me a kiss of greeting. She has kissed my feet again and again. You didn't honor me with olive oil to anoint my head. She has anointed my feet with perfume. Yes, she has many sins, but they've been forgiven. This is why she has shown me so much love."

The woman knew she was a sinner. This is why she loved Jesus so much. Simon didn't think he was a sinner. He thought he didn't need the Lord.

Dear God, help me to remember how much I need you.

HEALING ON THE SABBATH

Then he asked them, "If one of you has a son or an ox that falls into a well on the Sabbath day, will you not immediately pull him out?" And they had nothing to say.
LUKE 14:5–6 NIV

The religious leaders were always watching Jesus. They wanted to see if he did anything wrong. To them, it was against the law to work on Saturday. They called this day the Sabbath. So they especially watched to see what he did on the Sabbath.

One Sabbath day, Jesus was in the home of a religious leader. Everyone was watching him closely. They knew that a man was there whose arms and legs were badly swollen. Would Jesus heal him?

Jesus asked the religious leaders, "Tell me, does your law allow healing on the Sabbath day?" They wouldn't answer. So Jesus touched the sick man and he was healed. In case the religious leaders would be mad at the healed man, Jesus sent him home. Then Jesus turned to the watchers. "Don't you work on the Sabbath? What would you do if your donkey or your cow fell into a pit? Wouldn't you get him out right away?" Jesus knew they would, but they didn't answer him.

The Lord healed that man on the Sabbath because he loved him. The religious leaders had lost their love for people. They said they wouldn't work on the Sabbath for any reason. But they'd rescue their donkey because it was worth money.

Dear God, thank you for loving your people more than anything else.

THE LOST SON

"We must celebrate with a feast, for this son of mine was dead and has now returned to life. He was lost, but now he is found."
LUKE 15:23–24 NLT

A man had two sons. The younger one told his father, "I want my share of your money now, instead of waiting until you die." So the father divided his wealth between his sons.

A few days later, the younger son packed up and took a long vacation. He wasted all of his money and lived a wild life. Then his money ran out, and he began to starve. He got a job feeding pigs, but he was so hungry that even the pigs' food looked good to him.

The son finally came to his senses. "At home, even the servants have food to eat," he said. So he went home to his father.

The father saw his son coming from far away. He was filled with love for his son, and he ran to him and hugged and kissed him. His son said, "Father, I've sinned against you. I shouldn't be called your son anymore." But his father put the finest clothes on him. He put a ring on his finger and sandals on his feet. The whole household celebrated with a feast. "My son was dead and has returned to life," he said with joy. "He was lost. But now he is found."

Jesus told this story to show how much God loves us.

Dear God, thank you for your love and forgiveness.

THANKSGiVING

One of them, when he saw that he was healed,
came back to Jesus, shouting, "Praise God, I'm healed!"
He fell face down on the ground at Jesus' feet,
thanking him for what he had done.
LUKE 17:15–16 NLT

Here in the United States we have a holiday we call Thanksgiving. It's a day when we give thanks to God for all we have. Here's a story about thanksgiving:

One day, Jesus was near Samaria. In a village there, ten lepers stood crying out, "Jesus, have mercy on us!" He looked at them and said, "Go see the priests." And as they went, their leprosy disappeared.

One of them came back to Jesus shouting, "Praise God, I'm healed!" He fell at Jesus' feet, giving thanks.

"Didn't I heal ten men?" Jesus asked. "Where are the other nine?" Then he said to the man, "Stand up and go. Your faith has made you well."

This story shows that not many people give thanks to God. But the Bible says, "Let your lives overflow with thanksgiving for all he has done." Remember to thank God for everything. You'll feel great, and God will be happy.

Dear God, help me to remember to thank you for everything!

AVOIDING TROUBLE

Jesus called in a loud voice, "Lazarus, come out!"
The dead man came out, his hands and feet wrapped with strips of linen,
and a cloth around his face. Jesus said to them,
"Take off the grave clothes and let him go."
JOHN 11:43–44 NIV

Jesus did the greatest miracle and brought Lazarus back to life. As you would expect, many of the people saw this and believed in Jesus. But others went to the religious leaders and told them what Jesus had done.

The leaders got together to talk it over. "What shall we do?" they asked. "If we leave him alone, everyone will believe in him." They were afraid they would lose control over the people. From that day on, they tried to figure out how to kill Jesus. If anyone knew where Jesus was, they were ordered to tell the leaders.

So what did Jesus do? He did what anyone would do. He didn't live in the open among the Jews anymore. He went to a little town called Ephraim near the desert. He and his followers stayed there. Although he was God and could do anything, he lived as a man. It wasn't time for him to die yet. So he did the smart thing and stayed away from trouble.

Dear God, thank you for protecting Jesus. Please protect me, too.

GOD'S LIGHT

"The Pharisee stood up and prayed about himself: .
'God, I thank you that I am not like all other men. . . .'
But the tax collector. . .beat his breast and said,
'God, have mercy on me, a sinner.'
I tell you that this man, rather than the other,
went home justified before God.
For everyone who exalts himself will be humbled,
and he who humbles himself will be exalted."
LUKE 18:11—14 NIV

Have you ever walked around your neighborhood at night? Some houses have lights on inside and others don't. People in houses with lights on cannot see out into the dark. But a person in a room without light can easily see you walking in the street.

This story is about two men's prayers. One is a publican, which is a tax collector. The other is a Pharisee, which is a religious leader. The tax collector in the story could not see other people's faults. God had turned on the lights in his heart. The religious leader, however, had no light in his heart. It was as if he were sitting in a darkened room. He could not see himself; he just looked outside at others.

The religious leader knew the Bible. The tax collector did not. The religious leader had a special place in the temple. The tax collector stood at the edge of gathering. It is good to know the Bible and have a special place in church, but the religious leader mostly needed what the tax collector had. That is God's light.

Dear God, help me to see myself—not other people's faults.

ZACCHAEUS

There was a man there named Zacchaeus. . . .
He tried to get a look at Jesus, but he was too short to see over the crowds.
So he ran ahead and climbed a sycamore tree beside the road.
LUKE 19:2–4 NLT

In our country, many people love celebrities like movie stars and rock singers. These famous people are usually good looking. They are often tall and well dressed. You don't see very many short or ugly celebrities. But God doesn't care what anyone looks like. What matters most to God is your heart. He wants you to love him and seek him, just like Zacchaeus did.

Here's how Zacchaeus met the Lord. Jesus was traveling to Jerusalem for the last time. He passed through Jericho, where Zacchaeus lived. Zacchaeus was an important tax collector in town, so he was very rich. He wanted to see Jesus as He passed by. But Zacchaeus was too short to see over the crowds. So he ran ahead and climbed a sycamore tree beside the road. He could watch from there.

Zacchaeus probably looked silly in that tree. He was a grown man and a rich man, too. But he didn't care what people thought of him. He just wanted to see Jesus. When Jesus came by, he saw Zacchaeus in the tree and called him by name. "Zacchaeus!" he said. "Quick, come down! I want to stay in your home today."

Of all the people crowding the street that day, Jesus saw Zacchaeus. Why? Because Zacchaeus so badly wanted to see the Lord.

Dear God, I want to be like Zacchaeus—help me always to look for you!

GIVE TO GOD WHAT IS GOD'S

He said to them,
"Then give to Caesar what is Caesar's, and to God what is God's."
LUKE 20:25 NIV

As you know, the religious leaders wanted to arrest Jesus. They sent secret agents to him pretending to be honest men. They tried to get Jesus to say something wrong so they could arrest him. These spies said, "Teacher, you teach what is right and you don't care what others think. You only teach the ways of God. Please tell us this: Is it right to pay taxes to the Roman government?"

Jesus wasn't tricked. "Show me a Roman coin," he said. "Whose picture is on it?"

"Caesar's," they replied. Caesar was the king of Rome.

"Okay," he said, "give to Caesar what belongs to him. But give to God what belongs to God."

They failed again to trap him. In fact, they were amazed at what he said and kept their mouths shut.

You may remember that God made men and women to look like him. The coin had a picture of Caesar on it. So it belonged to Caesar. But we look like God. So we belong to God and shouldn't give ourselves to anyone else.

Dear God, help me not to give myself to anyone but you.

THE GOOD SHEPHERD

And wherever he went, he healed people of every sort of disease
and illness. He felt great pity for the crowds that came. . . .
They were like sheep without a shepherd.
MATTHEW 9:35–36 NLT

Jesus was born in Israel because he was a Jew. He loves all people,
but he first came to his own people—the Jews. To God, they are
like a flock of sheep. Jesus came to
be their shepherd and bring them
back to God. The leaders of Israel
at the time only took care of themselves. God's sheep had no shepherd.

Long before Jesus came, a man
named Ezekiel asked them:

"Shouldn't you shepherds take
care of God's people? You have all
you need, but you don't take care of
the flock. You haven't strengthened
the weak, healed the sick, or band-
aged the injured. You haven't brought back the stray sheep or
searched for the lost. You've ruled Israel harshly and brutally. They
were scattered because there was no shepherd. Then they became
food for wild animals. My sheep wandered all over the mountains
and on every hill. They were scattered over the whole earth, and no
one searched or looked for them."

This is why Jesus came. He said, "I have come to seek and save
those who are lost." He is the Good Shepherd who loves all people.

Dear God, thank you for being the Good Shepherd.

BETTER THAN SPARROWS

"Are not two sparrows sold for a penny?
Yet not one of them will fall to the ground apart from the will of your Father."
MATTHEW 10:29 NIV

God loves people more than anything else in Creation. We are the highest, best, and most important creatures. In Psalm 8, David wrote, "I think of your heavens, the work of your fingers, the moon and the stars. Out of all these, what is man, that you are mindful of him? You've made him a little lower than the angels. You've crowned him with glory and honor." This psalm says that all things are under our feet, meaning we are in charge. We control all things God created. We have control over all the animals on the ground, the birds of the air, and the fish of the sea.

Matthew 10 says that God knows everything that happens to every creature he made. Sparrows are birds that aren't worth much. People usually don't keep sparrows for pets. They're a dull brown color and just fly around eating crumbs. But if just one sparrow falls to the ground, our heavenly Father knows about it. He cares for every creature, even ones that don't seem to be important. How much must God care for human beings who are the center of his purpose?

Dear God, thank you for caring so much about me.

GOD KNOWS EVERYTHING

"And even the very hairs of your head are all numbered."

MATTHEW 10:30 NIV

The reason God knows everything about you is that he loves you. When a sparrow falls to the ground, God knows it. He also knows the number of hairs on your head. You have many thousands of hairs on your head, and God has counted them all.

God also keeps track of the number of hairs on your head. Throughout the day, here and there, one of your hairs falls out to the ground. Each time this happens, God still knows the number of hairs you have. That's how much God cares for you—he keeps track of every hair on your head!

People say that God is omnipotent, meaning God knows everything. This is true. Psalm 147:4 says, "God decides the number of the stars and calls each of them by name." Think about that. Every single star that you see shining in the sky has a name given by God. God is amazing!

Dear God, thank you for knowing everything about me—even the number of hairs on my head!

CAN'T PLEASE EVERYONE

"To what can I compare this generation?
They are like children sitting in the marketplaces and calling out to others:
'We played the flute for you, and you did not dance;
we sang a dirge and you did not mourn.'"
MATTHEW 11:16–17 NIV

In the days of Jesus, there was a man named John. He was sent by God to introduce Jesus to the people of Israel. John told them that Jesus was the Lamb of God who would die for their sins. Jesus said that John was the greatest prophet who ever lived. But the people didn't listen to John.

When Jesus came, the people didn't listen to him, either. So he told them they were like children in the town square playing games. One of them complained, "We played wedding music for you and you wouldn't dance." Another said, "We played funeral songs but you weren't sad." This was Jesus' way of saying that nothing would please the people.

John didn't drink wine, and he ate very simple food. Sometimes he ate nothing and only prayed. Yet people said, "He has an evil spirit."

Jesus, on the other hand, enjoyed plenty of good food and drink. What do you think the people said about him? "He eats too much. He's a drunkard and makes friends with the worst sinners!"

John and Jesus were sent by God to bring the wisdom of the gospel. Israel didn't listen to them. But in time, the gospel had marvelous results.

Dear God, help me to listen and please only you.

REST IN JESUS

"Come to me, all you who are weary and burdened, and I will give you rest.
Take my yoke upon you and learn from me,
for I am gentle and humble in heart, and you will find rest for your souls.
For my yoke is easy and my burden is light."

MATTHEW 11:28–30 NIV

Read these helpful verses when you are worried. Think of them when you must do something hard to do. At such times, take Jesus' invitation. Go to him and he'll give you rest.

Jesus said we should take his yoke. What is a yoke? Before there were tractors, farmers' plows were pulled by animals. Sometimes two oxen were used. Oxen are big strong cattle that were joined together with a yoke. This heavy, wooden bar fit around the oxen's necks to pull the plow. Because of the yoke, the oxen pulled together and shared the work. When you take Jesus' yoke, he is beside you pulling, too.

Jesus said he is gentle and humble. Oxen are like this. Although they're huge animals and very strong, they're quiet and gentle. Don't be afraid of being yoked beside Jesus. He won't hurt you. In fact, when you're in his yoke, you'll find rest for your soul.

If you're working, how can you be resting? How can your work be light instead of heavy? Because Jesus is so much stronger than us. He does all the work. When we are walking with him, we are not really working. While he's working, we're resting.

Dear God, thank you that I can find rest in Jesus.

THINK MORE

Going on from that place, he went into their synagogue,
and a man with a shriveled hand was there.
Looking for a reason to accuse Jesus, they asked him,
"Is it lawful to heal on the Sabbath?"

MATTHEW 12:9–10 NIV

Jesus went into a synagogue, where people heard the scriptures read and worshiped God. This was the Sabbath day. The Sabbath was very important to the Jewish people. It was their day of rest when they did no work. Women couldn't even light a fire to cook food. This was considered work by the Jewish religion. So people ate leftovers on the Sabbath.

On this Sabbath day, a handicapped man was at the synagogue. His hand was useless and shriveled up. The man's hand was probably small and wrinkled like an old piece of fruit. There was no life flowing through it.

The men teaching in the synagogue tried to trick Jesus. Remember, it was the Sabbath day, so no one could work. Jesus was asked if healing this man's hand would be considered work. Jesus was very wise and asked them a question of his own.

Someday this may happen when you ask God a question. Instead of an answer, God will give you another question. This is done for a reason: God wants you to think about things a little more.

Dear God, help me to know when I need to think and pray more.

DOING GOOD ON THE SABBATH

And he answered, "If you had one sheep, and it fell into a well on the Sabbath,
wouldn't you get to work and pull it out?
Of course you would.
And how much more valuable is a person than a sheep!
Yes, it is right to do good on the Sabbath."
MATTHEW 12:11—12 NLT

The men teaching in the synagogue asked Jesus a trick question about the Sabbath.

In return, Jesus asked them about a man and a sheep. "What should a man do if his sheep fell into a pit on the Sabbath day? Should he lift it out?"

Their answer was, "Yes, the man would probably save his sheep."

To lift the sheep out of the pit was work, and work was against the Sabbath law. But the man needed his sheep. So he would save it, even on the Sabbath. The sheep's life is more important than the Sabbath law.

So Jesus asked, "How much then is a man better than a sheep?" Jesus proved that it was right to heal a man on the Sabbath.

Jesus told the man to stretch out his hand. When he did, his hand was no longer withered! It was strong and full of life like his other hand. The man had two good hands. He must have been happy that Jesus would heal him on the Sabbath. This story shows how much God loves all people.

Dear God, thank you for loving people much more than any rules.

HE CARES ABOUT YOU

"A bruised reed he will not break,
and a smoldering wick he will not snuff out."
MATTHEW 12:20 NIV

When you're weak or heartbroken, you're like a bruised reed. But Jesus loves you. He won't break a bruised reed.

The stems of reeds are hollow. Ancient people used them as flutes. But they're delicate and easily damaged. A damaged flute could not make pretty music, so it was thrown away. A flute player could easily make a new reed flute.

Many things can bruise us, like accidents and disease. You may be strong, but pretend that you're a bruised reed and that Jesus is a flute player. Would he throw you away? No. He won't break a reed that can't make music. Jesus doesn't care if you can do anything for him. He simply cares about *you*.

After Jesus rose from the dead, his followers were afraid. They may have thought they would be killed, too. Jesus went to them in the locked room where they were hiding. He didn't throw them away just because they were afraid. "Peace be with you," he said. Then he breathed into them as if they were reed flutes. Jesus said, "Receive the Holy Spirit."

Bruised people can receive God's breath like a flute. This breath is the Holy Spirit to strengthen and cheer you.

Dear God, thank you for using me, no matter what my condition.

WHEN WE'RE WEAK

"A bruised reed he will not break,
and a smoldering wick he will not snuff out."
MATTHEW 12:20 NIV

Jesus won't break a bruised reed. He won't quench a smoldering wick, either. A wick is the piece of cloth that's inside a kerosene lamp. These were made of flax in Jesus' day. When it is lit, a lamp gives light. But a smoldering wick doesn't give clear light. Plus, it's smoky.

Pretend you're the wick in a lamp that's smoldering and giving off dim light. In other words, you're not perfect. Maybe you're sick or hurt in some way, or people don't like you or want you. But Jesus doesn't put out your light. He knows you're not perfect, no matter how hard you try.

Paul helped to write the Bible. But he was a bruised and smoldering person. He was the leading sinner before he became a Christian. But the Lord told him, "My grace is all you need. My power works best in weak people."

Then Paul said, "I'm happy to be weak and troubled. Then I have Christ's power in me."

So when you're weak, Jesus doesn't cut you off like a smoldering wick. Instead, he himself becomes your light. In other words, he becomes your strength, just as he was in Paul.

Dear God, I know I am weak. Please make me strong with your power.

THE ONLY MIRACLE WE NEED

"A wicked and adulterous generation asks for a miraculous sign!
But none will be given it except the sign of the prophet Jonah.
For as Jonah was three days and three nights in the belly of a huge fish,
so the Son of Man will be three days and three nights in the heart of the earth."
MATTHEW 12:39–40 NIV

Jesus had done many miracles. He'd healed people of diseases and given sight to the blind. Still, many people asked him to do more miracles. These people didn't believe in Jesus even after seeing all his miracles.

Jesus told them that they would see only one more miracle. He called it the sign of Jonah. Do you know the story of Jonah? He was swallowed by some kind of big fish or whale. He was alive in the belly of that fish, if you can imagine that! Jonah was there for three days and three nights. Then God made the fish vomit Jonah up on the beach. Jesus said the people would see this miracle. What does it mean?

The sign of Jonah is Jesus' own death and resurrection. The same people who asked for more miracles would one day kill Jesus. He was buried, but three days later he arose from the dead, like Jonah came out of the fish. This is called resurrection. It is the greatest of all miracles and the only one we need.

Even when Jesus was resurrected, many people didn't believe. They said, "He didn't rise from the grave. His followers stole his body."

Dear God, thank you that Jesus died and rose again—the only miracle we need.

THE PARABLE OF THE SOWER

*"The good soil represents the hearts of those who truly accept
God's message and produce a huge harvest—thirty, sixty,
or even a hundred times as much as had been planted."*
MATTHEW 13:23 NLT

Jesus talked about ordinary things to teach people about God. He didn't try to confuse anyone. He wanted the invisible, spiritual things to be clear so that we could understand them. He also gave ordinary acts spiritual meaning so that our lives could remind us of God.

The parable of the sower is about a farmer planting seed. But this was not a vegetable garden, where seeds are planted one by one. This farmer was in a big field planting wheat. He carried a bag of seed over his shoulder. He dipped his big hand into the seed and tossed the seed onto the land. The seed landed on hard earth, in stony ground, in the weeds, or in good earth.

Later, Jesus explained this story. He said that the ground is your heart and the seed is God's Word. Some hearts are hard. The truth of God can't even start growing there. Hearts with no room for Jesus are like ground filled with stones or weeds.

So you might wonder about your heart. Can the seed of the Word grow there? Simply pray every day that God will soften your heart. Ask the Lord to remove the stones and weeds. The Lord will do this, and then the Word of God can grow in you!

Dear God, please soften my heart and let your Word grow in me!

TREASURE

*"The Kingdom of Heaven is like a treasure that a man discovered hidden in a field.
In his excitement, he hid it again and sold everything he owned to get
enough money to buy the field—and to get the treasure, too!"*

MATTHEW 13:44 NLT

My wife lived out in the country when she was a child. There, she rode her horse on back roads where there were few cars. One day from astride her horse, she saw something green lying in the grass. *Maybe it's a dollar bill!* she thought. Jumping down from her horse, she found it was a ten-dollar bill! That was a lot of money to her, and she was excited to find it. She hadn't even been looking for it. The money was a treasure to her.

Jesus tells us that his kingdom is like a treasure. It's a treasure hidden in a field. A man finds this treasure and decides to buy the field. He knows if he owns the field, he owns the wonderful treasure in it.

This is what Jesus did. The field is the world and the treasure is God's kingdom. Jesus gave everything he had when he died on the cross. His death was the payment that bought the whole world for God. Now that Jesus owns the world, he also owns the treasure in the world. That treasure is everyone who is in God's kingdom.

Dear God, thank you that I am a treasure to you.

THE SON OF GOD

When Jesus came to the region of Caesarea Philippi, he asked his disciples,
"Who do people say the Son of Man is?"
MATTHEW 16:13 NIV

Jesus went to a place called Caesarea Philippi. The Jordan River springs from the hills of this faraway place. Jesus took his followers there on a retreat. He asked them this question: "Who do people say I am?"

They had a few answers to this:

"Some say you are John the Baptist." John was the man who prepared the way for Jesus' coming.

"Some people say you are Elijah." This was Israel's greatest prophet who lived hundreds of years before Jesus.

"Others say you are Jeremiah or one of the other prophets."

These were all good answers but they were wrong. People thought Jesus was other things, too. They said he was a drunkard, a rebel, a heretic, and a criminal. To others he was a healer, a feeder of the hungry, a miracle worker, and more.

But Jesus wanted a different answer than these. So he asked them, "Who do *you* say that I am?"

Peter spoke up, "You are the Christ, the Son of the Living God."

Hurrah! Someone finally got it right. Jesus is the Son of God.

"Peter," Jesus said, "you are blessed. You did not learn this from anyone other than my Father in heaven."

Dear God, thank you for being who you are.

FINISHING GOD'S PLAN

As the men watched, Jesus' appearance changed so that his face shone like the sun, and his clothing became dazzling white.

MATTHEW 17:2 NLT

Jesus Christ was God who came to live with us as a man. He looked like an ordinary man. Everyone knew he came from a town called Nazareth. This was just an ordinary place. He was raised in a carpenter's home with brothers and sisters. Nearly no one knew that Jesus was God.

One day, Jesus went with three of his followers to the top of a mountain. There, Peter, James, and John saw something that no one had seen before. They saw Jesus as God. His face shone like the sun and his body was white light.

Just then, two other men appeared with Jesus. Both of them had lived hundreds of years before. One was Moses, the great leader of Israel. The other was Elijah the prophet. Peter wanted to set up tents to worship Moses, Elijah, and Jesus. But God put a stop to this saying, "This is my beloved Son, and I am fully pleased with him. Listen to him."

This happened so people would know that the old way was past. There was no reason to worship anyone other than Jesus. Moses and Elijah had done their jobs. Now Jesus would finish God's plan.

Dear God, thank you for sending Jesus to finish your plan.

JESUS ONLY

Just then there appeared before them Moses and Elijah, talking with Jesus.
Peter said to Jesus, "Lord, it is good for us to be here. If you wish,
I will put up three shelters—one for you, one for Moses and one for Elijah."
MATTHEW 17:3–4 NIV

Something more happened on that mountain. Two men that had lived thousands of years before were there talking with Jesus. They were Moses and Elijah. When Peter saw them, he blurted out, "Let's make three shelters!" In these, they could worship Moses, Elijah, and Jesus. It was as if he thought the three of them were equal. But they weren't. Peter forgot that Jesus is the Son of God. Moses and Elijah were only God's prophets.

Suddenly a cloud came over them. God wanted Peter to know the truth. He spoke from the cloud, "This is my Son, whom I love. I am pleased with him. So listen to him!"

What would you do if you heard God's voice shouting from a cloud? Peter, James, and John were afraid and fell on the ground. But God didn't want to frighten them. Jesus came to his friends and touched them. He was a real, living, tender human being. He comforted them. When they looked up, Moses and Elijah were gone. They only saw the man Jesus. They had learned that Jesus is the only one who tells the truth about God.

Dear God, help me to only worship you.

DON'T BE AFRAID TO GIVE

Then a poor widow came and dropped in two pennies.
[Jesus] called his disciples to him and said, "I assure you,
this poor widow has given more than all the others have given.
For they gave a tiny part of their surplus, but she,
poor as she is, has given everything she has."

MARK 12:42–44 NLT

In the ancient temple, money was collected to give to the poor. This poor widow who gave all her money at the temple is like another widow in the Bible.

The prophet Elijah went to a town called Zarephath. There he saw a widow gathering sticks. He asked her, "Would you bring me a cup of water and a bite of bread?"

"I'll tell you the truth," she answered. "I have no bread in my house. I do have a handful of flour left in the jar and a little cooking oil in the bottom of the jug. I was gathering a few sticks to cook my last meal. Then my son and I will die."

Elijah told her, "Don't be afraid. Cook your meal, but first bake a loaf of bread for me. There will be enough food for you. The Lord tells me you will have flour and oil left over."

The widow did this, and she, Elijah, and her son ate for many days. No matter how much flour and oil they used, there was always enough left over.

These two widows teach us to not be afraid to give to others. When we do, God will take care of everything we need.

Dear God, help me to give to others as the widow and her son did.

GiViNG TO JESUS

During supper, a woman came in with a beautiful jar of expensive perfume.
She broke the seal and poured the perfume over his head.
MARK 14:3 NLT

Have you ever wondered if you should believe in Jesus? Here is a story about a woman who believed in Jesus and gave all she had to him.

Jesus was in Bethany at the home of Simon the Leper. During supper, a woman came in with a beautiful jar of expensive perfume. She opened it and poured the perfume over Jesus' head. Some of those eating with him were angry. "What a waste!" they said. "She could have sold that perfume for a small fortune. The money should have gone to the poor!" Then they scolded the woman.

"Leave her alone," said Jesus. "Why scold her for doing a good thing to Me? You will always have the poor to take care of. You can help them whenever you want to. But I won't be with you much longer. She's done what she could and has prepared my body for burial early. Believe me, wherever the gospel is preached, what this woman has done will be remembered."

It is never a waste to give yourself to Jesus.

Dear God, help me to give all that I have to you.

LIKE A CHILD

*"I tell you the truth, unless you change and become like little children,
you will never enter the kingdom of heaven."*
MATTHEW 18:3 NIV

Children are eager to learn. In the kingdom, adults are the same.
They only want to know God and learn all about the Lord's ways.
Many adults aren't in the kingdom, though. They work hard all the

time for money with no time for
God. But children are different.
They love God and have simple
faith in him.

In the kingdom, adults are like
children—thankful and living
with a happy heart. God doesn't
want people to work to be greater
than everyone else. Instead, God
wants to be the greatest in everyone's hearts.

This was not an easy lesson for
Jesus' disciples to learn. They once
saw parents bring their children to Jesus so he could pray for them.
The disciples tried to push the children out of the way. They told
their parents to leave Jesus alone. But Jesus asked the children to
come to him. He probably gave them a hug and told them how
much he loved them.

Remember, even though you're young and small, you are important to Jesus. Right now, he is in heaven praying for you.

Dear God, thank you for loving children like me.

LOST SHEEP

*"In the same way your Father in heaven is not willing
that any of these little ones should be lost."*

MATTHEW 18:14 NIV

Remember, God's people are like sheep. Jesus told this story about a shepherd and his sheep:

A shepherd had a hundred sheep. He brought them all into the barn. Then he discovered that he only had ninety-nine sheep. One of his precious sheep was missing! This shepherd didn't say, "Oh, well, who cares? I have enough sheep. Ninety-nine is plenty. I don't want to go out and look for one lost sheep." No, the shepherd loved all his sheep. So he left his ninety-nine sheep safely in the barn. He then climbed back up the mountain to find his lost sheep. He looked all over the mountainside until he found it. When the lost sheep was found, everyone was happy.

Jesus is the real Shepherd and we are his real sheep. He won't let any of us be lost. He always finds each of us and brings us back to the flock. Many people in this world have lost their way. The world is like a dark, rainy, cold mountainside. On it, people are wandering because they've lost their way. But Jesus, the Good Shepherd, can bring each of them back to God.

Dear God, thank you for loving and finding your lost sheep.

THE LAST WILL BE FIRST

"He answered one of them, 'Friend, I haven't been unfair!
Didn't you agree to work all day for the usual wage?
Take it and go. I wanted to pay this last worker the same as you.' "
MATTHEW 20:13–14 NLT

Early one morning, a farmer hired men to work in his vineyard. Later that morning, he passed through town and saw men doing nothing. So he hired them. Twice more he did the same thing.

At five o'clock, the farmer saw more men standing around. He asked them, "Why haven't you been working today?"

"No one hired us," they told him.

"Then go on out and work with the others in my vineyard."

When the day was done, he paid the workers. They all got a full day's pay. The men who were hired early complained, "Those people worked only one hour. Yet you've paid them just as much as you paid us. And we worked all day!"

"Friends," he answered, "I wanted to pay the last workers the same as you. Is this against the law? Should you be angry because I am kind?"

This story tells about the kingdom of heaven. In it, the last will be first and the first will be last. In other words, there is no first and there is no last. We're all the same in God's eyes. We all get the same pay; we all get God. In the end, God will be everything to every one of us.

Dear God, thank you for being everything to me.

VINE AND BRANCHES

"Yes, I am the vine; you are the branches.
Those who remain in me, and I in them, will produce much fruit.
For apart from me you can do nothing."
JOHN 15:5 NLT

Have you ever seen a grapevine? Jesus once said that he was like a grapevine. The branches on this vine are all the believers in Jesus. Are the vine and the branches separate? No. Can the branches live without the vine? No. The branches depend on the vine.

Inside a grapevine, sap flows just like inside a tree. Just like this sap brings life to the branches, Jesus brings life to us. We aren't just friends of Jesus. We are not doing business with God. When we believe in Jesus, something amazing happens. His life begins to flow to us like sap in a vine. All the Lord asks is that we stay connected to the vine. Then, like branches of a grapevine, we will bear fruit for him. But our fruit is not grapes. Our fruit is a way of life. In our life we will find the fruits of the Spirit—love, joy, peace, patience, kindness, goodness, faithfulness, gentleness, and self-control.

Dear God, I want to grow good fruit—let Jesus flow through my life!

THE BLIND SEE

"Lord," they said, "we want to see!" Jesus felt sorry for them and touched their eyes.
Instantly they could see! Then they followed him.

MATTHEW 20:33–34 NLT

When Jesus was leaving Jericho, a large crowd followed him. It must have been very noisy and confusing. Amidst all that chaos, two men sat by the roadside. The crowd was all around them, even stepping on top of them. The two men were blind, but they knew

that Jesus was passing by. They shouted at the top of their lungs to be heard above the noise, "Have mercy on us!"

The crowd didn't care about the two blind men. They told them to be quiet. But the blind men didn't do it; they shouted even louder to Jesus, "Have mercy on us!"

Jesus heard them and stopped. He stood very still. The crowd must have stopped and stood still, too. What would Jesus do about these shouting blind men? He politely asked, "What do you want?"

"Lord, open our eyes."

Jesus touched their eyes.

The blind men could see! But they didn't run off to look at all the pretty things in the world. They could see Jesus! He had given them their sight. The giver is always more important than the gift. Gifts are good, but the giver is the best. So they followed the Lord.

Dear God, thank you for making the blind to see.

HUMBLE LIKE JESUS

Jesus sent two disciples, saying to them,
"Go to the village ahead of you, and at once you will find a donkey tied there,
with her colt by her. Untie them and bring them to me."
MATTHEW 21:1–2 NIV

Jesus seems to have walked nearly everywhere he went. But just before he died, there was a big celebration in Jerusalem in his honor. That day, Jesus sent two of his disciples into a village to find a donkey to ride. A mother donkey there had a little colt with her. The disciples brought them to Jesus.

They had no beautiful scarves or cloth to decorate the animals. Their everyday cloaks would have to do. Jesus got onto the donkey with a saddle of cloaks and rode into Jerusalem.

Donkeys aren't tall and beautiful like horses. They're small and homely with big ears and dull gray-brown hair. Imagine the Lord riding on a little donkey. His legs would have hung down almost to the ground. He probably looked silly that day. But Jesus didn't care. Instead, the words of an old prophet named Zechariah came true: "Rejoice greatly, O people of Zion! Shout in triumph, O people of Jerusalem! Look, your king is coming to you. He is righteous and victorious, yet he is humble, riding on a donkey—even on a donkey's colt."

Dear God, help me to be humble, just like Jesus was.

THE TRIUMPHAL ENTRY

The next day, the news that Jesus was on the way to Jerusalem swept through the city. A huge crowd of Passover visitors took palm branches and went down the road to meet him. They shouted, "Praise God!"

JOHN 12:12–13 NLT

This is the beginning of the last week of Jesus' life on the earth.

He and his followers were in a town called Bethphage, near Jerusalem. "Go into the village over there," he told two of his followers. "You'll see a donkey there, with its colt beside it. Untie them and bring them here."

The two did as Jesus said and brought the donkeys to him. They threw their coats over the little colt, and Jesus sat on it and rode into Jerusalem.

When Jesus was born, he was called the King of the Jews. You'd think he would ride into the city on a beautiful, tall horse. After all, he was the king! Instead, he rode on a baby donkey.

Hundreds of years before, a man predicted this would happen.

He wrote, "Tell the people of Israel, 'Look, your king is coming to you. He is humble, riding on a donkey—even on a donkey's colt.' "

A crowd was waiting for Jesus in Jerusalem. They spread their coats on the road ahead of him. Others cut branches from the trees and spread them on the road. The crowds all around him shouted, "Praise God for the Son of David! Praise God in highest heaven!"

Dear God, thank you so much for your son, Jesus Christ, and all he has done!

A HUMBLE KING

This was done to fulfill the prophecy,
"Tell the people of Israel,
'Look, your King is coming to you.
He is humble, riding on a donkey—
even on a donkey's colt.' "
MATTHEW 21:4–5 NLT

In these days, rich and important men ride in fancy cars. They like long, expensive limousines with special uniformed drivers.

Jesus was God and the most important man who ever lived. Yet he was willing to ride into Jerusalem on a dusty donkey. He didn't choose an elegant white horse. He didn't gallop in on an excited, rearing stallion. Jesus is a humble king—a king willing to give his life for his people.

As Jesus rode into the city, people shouted praise and blessed his name. These people weren't rich or important people. They were probably like you and your family. They didn't have the money for a red carpet for Jesus to ride upon. They took off their rough, dull cloaks and threw them down on the ground. These were a carpet for their Lord. Nearby, palm trees were growing. The people broke off their branches and threw them on the ground, too. It was all they could do to show Jesus that they loved and honored him. This was enough for the humble king Jesus.

Dear God, help me to show Jesus that I love and honor him, too.

CLEARING OUT THE TEMPLE

He said, "The Scriptures declare, 'My Temple will be called a place of prayer,'
but you have turned it into a den of thieves!"
MATTHEW 21:13 NLT

What if you go to church next Sunday and someone is selling tickets? Someone has opened a bank there and people are lined up to get money. They use the money to pay their way into church. Inside the church, you find strangers selling religious items—decorations, books, and gifts. You can buy a hymnal and a Bible to use for worship. Cushions and chairs are available for rent. If you don't have one, you must stand. After the service, there are refreshments, but you have to pay for them. What would you do?

Would you do what Jesus did? He once saw salesmen selling animals to people who wanted to worship in the temple. They would use the animals as sacrifices. People couldn't worship unless they paid for an animal. Jesus was angry that God's house had been turned into a place to make money. So He drove out the salesmen and animals and turned over their tables and scattered their coins.

Only Jesus could do this because he is in charge of the church. You are in charge of your own heart. Like the church, it is also God's house. It is important to keep it clean and pure.

Dear God, help me to keep my heart pure for You.

DO WHAT YOU SAY

"But what do you think about this? A man with two sons told the older boy,
'Son, go out and work in the vineyard today.'
The son answered, 'No, I won't go,' but later he changed his mind
and went anyway. Then the father told the other son,
'You go' and he said, 'Yes, sir, I will.' But he didn't go.
Which of the two was obeying his father?"
MATTHEW 21:28—31 NLT

Suppose your mom asks you to clean your room. You say, "Sure, mom," but instead you go outside and play? How do you feel later when you see your mom's questioning look?

Another time, your mom asks you to load the dishwasher. You whine, "No, I don't want to." Yet, when she leaves, you go ahead and do it. How does your mother look when she sees the dishes are done? Doesn't her smiling face make you feel good that you helped her?

Which do you think is better? To say you'll do something and not do it, or to say you won't do something and then do it after all? It matters what you do, not what you say. To say you'll do something and then not do it makes your words worthless.

The religious leaders of Israel said they believed in God. They acted like they were holy and right. But when John the Baptist came preaching about Jesus, they didn't believe him. They didn't repent, and they weren't baptized. The sinners and tax collectors were very different from this. They didn't act holy; they knew they weren't living right. When John preached, the sinners believed. This made God happy.

Dear God, help me to do what I say and say what I do.

LEADING BY SERVING

It was just before the Passover Feast.
Jesus knew that the time had come
for him to leave this world and go to the Father.
Having loved his own who were in the world,
he now showed them the full extent of his love.
JOHN 13:1 NIV

The time came when Jesus would eat his last meal. "Go into Jerusalem," he told his followers. "There you'll see a man. Tell him I said that my time has come. We'll eat the meal at his house."

So they prepared supper in a room on the second floor of the man's house. That evening, Jesus sat down at the table with the twelve disciples.

Soon, he got up from the table, took off his robe, and wrapped a towel around his waist. He poured water into a big bowl. Then Jesus began to wash the disciples' feet. He wiped them dry with the towel. In those days, people wore sandals and their feet got dirty. At the end of the day, they'd wash their feet. But this time, Jesus did it for them. Isn't this odd? Jesus had spent three years teaching these men about God. They were his followers. Yet he stooped down to wash their feet. He was showing them that a real leader is one who serves others. The religious leaders wanted others to serve them, but that is not God's way. God wants us to serve like Jesus did.

Dear God, help me to serve others like Jesus did.

Communion

And he took bread, gave thanks and broke it, and gave it to them, saying,
"This is my body given for you; do this in remembrance of me."
In the same way, after the supper he took the cup, saying,
"This cup is the new covenant in my blood, which is poured out for you."

LUKE 22:19–20 NIV

Jesus didn't ask us to do very many things. But at his last supper, he told about the bread and cup. That night, the Lord Jesus took a loaf of bread. He gave thanks to God for it and broke it in pieces. He gave it to his followers. "This is my body, which is given for you," he said. "Remember me when you eat it."

After supper, Jesus took a cup of wine. "This cup is the new contract between God and you. My death is the signature on that contract. Remember me when you drink it."

That happened about two thousand years ago. People have been celebrating the Lord's Table ever since. You may have been at church when they have Communion. Churches do this because Jesus asked us to do it. It is not a fancy ceremony. There is a cup of wine or juice, a loaf of bread, and a few words. But it is the most meaningful thing we can do because we remember the Lord. We remember that he died for us. We remember that he is the bread of life. We remember that he is coming back. These things tell the story of God's love.

Dear God, thank you for Communion that helps us remember you.

ANGELS HELP JESUS

Then Jesus brought them to an olive grove called Gethsemane, and he said,
"Sit here while I go on ahead to pray."
MATTHEW 26:36 NLT

Jesus often took his followers to rest and pray in the Garden of Gethsemane. They were there praying on the night before Jesus died. The days before this night had made Jesus very tired. But the next day would be the hardest day of his life—the day he died. He was so weary that an angel came from heaven to help him.

You may have heard people talk of angels or seen pictures of angels. They don't often show up in Bible stories. Angels appear only when something very important is happening in God's plan. The most important thing that ever happened was Jesus' life. Angels were there right from the beginning. An angel told both Mary and Joseph about Jesus' birth.

Jesus once spent forty days alone in the wilderness. He didn't eat, but he prayed. When this time was over, angels came to help him. The next time angels appeared was here in Gethsemane. Angels were there when Jesus came back to life, too. There was an earthquake when an angel came to Jesus' grave. The Bible says this angel looked like lightning and his clothes were white as snow.

We shouldn't expect angels to appear again until Jesus comes back. Then, Jesus said, "I will come in the glory of my Father with his angels."

Dear God, help me to focus only on you and your son—and nothing else.

SAY YOU BELIEVE

"I tell you the truth," Jesus answered, "today—yes, tonight—before the rooster crows twice you yourself will disown me three times." But Peter insisted emphatically, "Even if I have to die with you, I will never disown you."

MARK 14:30–31 NIV

Peter was the leader among Jesus' followers. He was a strong, honest fisherman. But he did something surprising on the night Jesus was arrested. Here's the story:

The soldiers who arrested Jesus took him to the high priest's house. Peter was outside warming himself at a fire. One of the priest's servant girls noticed him there. She looked at him carefully and said, "You were with Jesus."

Peter said "I don't know what you're talking about." Just then, a rooster crowed.

The servant girl told the others, "That man is one of them!"

Peter denied it again.

Later, others said to Peter, "You must be one of them. You're from Galilee."

"I swear by God," he replied, "I don't know Jesus." Then the rooster crowed a second time. Suddenly, Peter remembered: "Before the rooster crows twice, you'll deny me three times." Peter wept with sorrow.

That was a hard night to admit to being a believer. All the other followers had run away; only Peter stayed near the Lord. Peter was probably afraid that he would be arrested, too. Still, we learn a lesson from him. It is always best to tell others that you believe in Jesus.

Dear God, help me not to be afraid to tell others about you.

ARRESTED!

Now Judas, who betrayed him, knew the place,
because Jesus had often met there with his disciples. So Judas came to the grove,
guiding a detachment of soldiers and some officials from the chief priests
and Pharisees. They were carrying torches, lanterns and weapons.
JOHN 18:2–3 NIV

The religious leaders looked for Jesus when he was away from the crowds. Then they could arrest him in secret. Finally, someone told

them where he was. It was Judas Iscariot, one of Jesus' close followers. They arrested Jesus in the garden at Gethsemane, where he was praying. The religious leaders took him to be judged by a man named Pilate, who was the governor of Israel.

Pilate ordered his soldiers to beat Jesus with a whip. Then they made a crown of long, sharp thorns and put it on Jesus' head. They also put a purple robe on him and made fun of him. "Hail! King of the Jews!" They laughed and hit him with their fists.

Pilate knew Jesus wasn't a criminal, but he took him outside wearing the thorny crown and the purple robe. He told the people, "Here is the man!"

The religious leaders and the guards shouted, "Crucify! Crucify!"

"You crucify him," Pilate said. "I don't think he's guilty."

The leaders told him, "By our laws he must die because he called himself the Son of God."

You see? Jesus wasn't killed because he'd done something wrong. He died because of who he was. He was and is the Son of God.

Dear God, thank you for your Son, Jesus.

THE DEATH OF JESUS

They crucified him, and with him two others—
one on each side and Jesus in the middle.
Pilate had a notice prepared and fastened to the cross. It read:
JESUS OF NAZARETH, THE KING OF THE JEWS.

JOHN 19:18–19 NIV

Jesus died because he was the Son of God. This is why God sent him to this world. The Bible says, "God so loved the world that he gave his only Son, so that everyone who believes in him will not perish but have eternal life. God did not send his Son into the world to condemn it, but to save it."

They took Jesus away to a place called Golgotha. There they nailed his arms and feet to a cross. He hung there until he died. Two other men were crucified with him. They were criminals. One was on either side with Jesus between them. Pilate nailed a sign over Jesus that read: JESUS OF NAZARETH, THE KING OF THE JEWS.

The soldiers stole Jesus' clothes. They took his robe and gambled to see who got it. Standing nearby were Jesus' mother; another woman named Mary; and Mary Magdalene.

When Jesus knew he was about to die, he said, "I'm thirsty." A jar of vinegar was there. They soaked a sponge in it, put it on a stick, and held it to his lips. Jesus tasted it and said, "It is finished!" Then he bowed his head and gave up his spirit.

Dear God, thank you giving up your only Son for us.

NEVER TOO LATE

Then he said, "Jesus, remember me when you come into your Kingdom."
And Jesus replied, "I assure you, today you will be with me in paradise."
LUKE 23:42–43 NLT

It is never too late to believe in Jesus. When Jesus died, two criminals were crucified with him. Each one hung on a cross. One was on Jesus' right side, the other on his left.

One of the criminals made fun of the Lord. "So you're the Messiah, are you?" he sneered. "Prove it! Save yourself, and save us, too."

But the other criminal didn't like this. "You're dying," he said to the mocking criminal. "Don't you fear God even now? We did evil things and deserve to die. But this man hasn't done anything wrong." Then he said, "Jesus, remember me when you come into your Kingdom."

Jesus replied, "I promise you, today you will be with me in paradise."

The criminal died that day. The last thing he did was to believe in Jesus, and now he is in paradise with him!

Dear God, thank you for accepting anyone who believes on you, no matter when.

RISEN!

At the place where Jesus was crucified, there was a garden,
and in the garden a new tomb, in which no one
had ever been laid. They laid Jesus there.

JOHN 19:41–42 NIV

They buried Jesus, but his death was not the end.

Early the next morning, one of Jesus' followers went to the tomb. Her name was Mary Magdalene. She saw that the stone had been rolled away from the door of the tomb. She was afraid. Did someone steal the body of her Lord? She ran and found Peter and John who also had followed Jesus. She said, "They've taken the Lord's body out of the tomb. I don't know where they've put him!"

The two men ran to the tomb and saw that Jesus' body was gone. Then they understood—he had risen from the dead!

Peter and John went home, but Mary stood there weeping. Then she saw two angels sitting where the body of Jesus had been.

"Why are you crying?" the angels asked.

"Because they've taken away my Lord," she replied. Then she glanced over her shoulder. Someone was standing behind her. It was Jesus! But Mary thought it was the gardener.

"Why are you crying?" Jesus asked

"Sir," she said, "Tell me where you've put him."

He said, "Mary."

She turned and called out, "Teacher!"

Mary Magdalene ran to tell Jesus' followers, "I have seen the Lord!"

Jesus was killed, and he was buried, but he rose from the dead, just like promised.

Dear God, thank you for Jesus' death and resurrection.

DAWNING AT THE TOMB

Early Sunday morning, while it was still dark,
Mary Magdalene came to the tomb and found that
the stone had been rolled away from the entrance.
JOHN 20:1 NLT

When he died, Jesus' body was covered with expensive spices and wrapped in linen cloth. Then it was laid in a small cave-like tomb. A huge boulder was rolled over its entrance. But Jesus didn't stay dead! He resurrected, or came back to life!

Early on the first day of the week, Mary Magdalene came to the tomb. She'd brought more spices for Jesus' body. She had no idea how she was going to move the big stone. Mary stood there, staring in shock. The heavy boulder had already been rolled away! There had been an earthquake and an angel had rolled the stone away. Mary ran as fast as she could to find Peter and John. She told them that someone had taken Jesus' body from the tomb.

Jesus had told his followers that he was going to rise from the dead, but none of them understood what he meant. But now, Peter and John were at Jesus' empty tomb. They realized Jesus was no longer dead, and they finally believed in him.

Dear God, thank you that Jesus rose from the dead.

DEVOTED TO JESUS

But Mary stood outside the tomb crying. As she wept,
she bent over to look into the tomb and saw two angels in white,
seated where Jesus' body had been, one at the head and the other at the foot.
JOHN 20:11–12 NIV

Peter and John left the empty tomb, but Mary Magdalene stayed there weeping. She loved Jesus so much. She had watched as he died on the cross. Now she'd found that his tomb was empty. Mary had no idea what had happened to the man she loved so much.

Mary bent to look into the tomb and saw two angels! They sat in the place where Jesus' body had been. One was at the head and one was at the foot.

They asked Mary, "Why are you crying?"

"They've taken my Lord, and I don't know where they've put him." Mary must have thought that someone had come in the night and moved Jesus' body to a different place.

Then Mary turned and saw a man standing there. She thought he was the gardener. "Tell me where you've carried Jesus," she said.

Suddenly, the man called her by her name, "Mary!"

Mary wiped away her tears. This wasn't the gardener. It was Jesus!

The most important thing we can do is to love the Lord. Mary Magdalene loved Jesus so much that she wouldn't leave his tomb. So she was the first person to see him after he rose from the dead.

Dear God, help me to love Jesus just like Mary Magdalene did.

PEACE BE WiTH YOU

On the evening of that first day of the week,
when the disciples were together,
with the doors locked for fear of the Jews,
Jesus came and stood among them and said,
"Peace be with you!"
JOHN 20:19 NIV

Mary Magdalene ran from the empty tomb. She found the disciples and told them that she'd seen the Lord.

That evening the disciples gathered in a room where all the doors were locked. By now many people probably knew that Jesus was gone from his tomb. Did they think the disciples had stolen his body away? The disciples thought they were in big trouble. Maybe they'd be killed like Jesus was! In the middle of all this fear, Jesus came into the room. How did he get into a locked room? No one knows. Jesus was not a ghost. He had a body that the disciples could see.

The Lord's first words to his fearful friends were, "Peace be with you."

Jesus had come to breathe the Holy Spirit into his disciples. Nothing could have been more important.

When the resurrected Christ breathed into his disciples, they changed. They became the temple of the living God. God no longer lived in the temple in Jerusalem. God has lived in human beings ever since.

Dear God, thank you for giving your Holy Spirit to live in us.

THE HOLY SPIRIT

He spoke to them again and said,
"Peace be with you. As the Father has sent me, so I send you."
Then he breathed on them and said to them, "Receive the Holy Spirit."
JOHN 20:21–22 NLT

Jesus' followers were afraid, confused, and very sad. They'd spent three years with Jesus, but suddenly he was gone. He'd been arrested and killed in a horrible way. They were afraid that they would be arrested, too. They were confused about what had happened and what to do next. And they were so sad that Jesus had died.

The followers were in a secret meeting two days after Jesus died. All the doors were closed for fear of the religious leaders. But all of a sudden Jesus stood with them saying, "Peace be with you."

Jesus' followers were overjoyed when they saw him. Again, he said, "Peace be with you." He didn't want them to be afraid of the religious leaders. He also didn't want them to be afraid of him. This was the first time they'd seen Jesus back to life.

Next, Jesus did the most wonderful thing imaginable. He breathed on them and said, "Receive the Holy Spirit." And so they did. From that day on, they were different because they had the Spirit of God inside them. He said, "I am with you always, even to the end of the age." As the Spirit, Jesus made his promise true.

Dear God, thank you for sending the Holy Spirit to live inside all believers.

DOUBTING THOMAS

Then he said to Thomas, "Put your finger here; see my hands.
Reach out your hand and put it into my side. Stop doubting and believe."
JOHN 20:27 NIV

When Jesus breathed the Holy Spirit into the disciples, they saw him and believed. But what about Thomas, who was not with the disciples that evening? When the disciples told him that they had seen the Lord, Thomas didn't believe them. To believe, he would have to see the nail marks in Jesus' hands. He said he had to put his finger into the nail holes and his hand into the opening in Jesus' side. "Otherwise," Thomas exclaimed, "I will not believe."

Eight days later, the disciples were together again in a locked room. This time Thomas was with them. Again, Jesus mysteriously came into the room. He had a special body called a resurrected body, a glorified body. He could come into a room where the doors were locked. But Thomas could also touch him and believe.

Jesus greeted his disciples, "Peace be with you." Then he told the doubting Thomas to put his fingers into the nail marks in His hands and put his hand into his side. Thomas no longer doubted. He proclaimed, "My Lord and my God!"

Dear God, help me never to doubt you.

BELIEVING WITHOUT SEEING

Then Jesus told him, "You believe because you have seen me.
Blessed are those who haven't seen me and believe anyway."
JOHN 20:29 NLT

After Thomas believed, Jesus gave a blessing. He blessed all the people who would ever believe in him. He said, "Blessed are those who haven't seen me and believe anyway." This includes you and me. You've never seen Jesus. You've never touched his physical body. Nor have you seen his resurrected, glorified body. Yet you believe in Him.

You love your mother. You see her everyday. She plays games with you and reads to you. She makes your meals and drives you to the park. It is easy to love her and believe she is real. You see her and experience all she does for you. Do you see Jesus? No. Do you believe in Jesus? Yes. Do you love Jesus? Yes. This is why Jesus says we are blessed. Even though we've never seen him, we still believe in him and love him.

Somehow, in your heart, you know him and believe in him. As the Bible says, "Although you have not seen him, you love him. Even though you do not see him now, you believe in him. This makes you rejoice with a glorious joy that is too wonderful for words."

Dear God, thank you for helping me believe in you, even though I cannot see you.

JESUS PROVIDES

Simon Peter said, "I'm going fishing."
"We'll come, too," they all said.
So they went out in the boat, but they caught nothing all night.
At dawn the disciples saw Jesus standing on the beach,
but they couldn't see who he was.
JOHN 21:3–4 NLT

Jesus came to his disciples a third time after he rose from the dead, when seven of the disciples were out fishing. They had been fishing all night but had caught nothing. This is odd because most of these men were skilled fishermen.

When dawn came, Jesus was standing on the shore. But the disciples didn't know who it was. Jesus called to them, "Children, do you have any fish?" No, they didn't have even one fish. So Jesus told them to cast their net to the right side of the boat. There they would find fish. They did this and caught so many fish they couldn't even lift the net!

Suddenly, John knew that the man on the beach was Jesus. "It's the Lord!" he yelled.

Peter was so excited to get to Jesus that he swam to shore. The others rowed the boat to shore dragging the net full of fish. When they arrived on the beach, Jesus had breakfast ready for them.

Yum, barbecued fish for breakfast! And bread, too. We never need to worry about what we'll eat. Jesus always provides for us.

Dear God, thank you for always providing for me.

NECESSARY FOOD

When they landed, they saw a fire of burning coals there with fish on it,
and some bread. Jesus said to them,
"Bring some of the fish you have just caught. . . .
Come and have breakfast."
JOHN 21:9–10, 12 NIV

After his death, Jesus spent forty days in resurrection with his followers.

Early one morning some of his followers were in their boat, fishing. They had fished all night and caught nothing. They looked up from their fishing nets and saw someone on the shore. Who could it be?

Jesus called to them, "Children, have you caught any fish?"

"No," they answered.

"Throw your net on the right side of the boat. There you'll find some."

They did this and caught so many fish they couldn't pull in the net! Just then, one of them understood who it was. He cried out, "It is the Lord!" They rushed to get to shore. There was a small fire. Fish were cooking on it and bread was nearby.

Jesus said to them, "Come, have breakfast."

Have you noticed how often Jesus served food to his followers? This was important to him. Food is a comfort. It helps people to be happy together. Without it we cannot live. Also, Jesus is food to us. He said he is the bread of life. He also gives us the water of life. He wants us to take him as our spiritual food and live by him.

Dear God, thank you for Jesus—our bread and water of life.

After his suffering, he showed himself to these men
and gave many convincing proofs that he was alive.
He appeared to them over a period of forty days
and spoke about the kingdom of God.
ACTS 1:3 NIV

For forty days, Jesus appeared to his disciples. He did this to teach them about the kingdom of God. Then he went with them to

Bethany. There he spoke to them his last words. He told them not to leave the city of Jerusalem. They were to wait there for the Father's promise. This is the powerful Holy Spirit, who would come back and make them strong. Then they would be able to preach and be witnesses for Jesus.

But the disciples were worried about something. *Had the time come when Jesus would be the king of Israel?* they wondered. They seem to have wanted this to happen right away.

But Jesus told them, "It is not for you to know this. Only the Father knows." Then he was taken up into the heavens. He went up until they lost sight of him in a cloud. As the disciples looked up, two men in white clothing appeared. These men must have been angels. They asked the disciples why they were staring up into the sky. Then the angels gave them wonderful news: Jesus will come back in the same way he left. Then the kingdom will come and Jesus will be king!

Dear God, thank you that Jesus will come back for us.

EXPECTING HIS RETURN

"Men of Galilee," they said, "why do you stand here looking into the sky?
This same Jesus, who has been taken from you into heaven,
will come back in the same way you have seen him go into heaven."
ACTS 1:11 NIV

The two angels promised that Jesus would come back for Israel. The Bible guarantees that this will come true. The Lord will come for the church, too. He'll come down from heaven with a shout. The archangel will call and a heavenly trumpet will sound. Then we who are alive on the earth will be caught up in the clouds. There we will meet the Lord in the air!

I know a woman who became a Christian over thirty years ago. She was a young woman then and had just finished college. That summer she worked hoeing weeds in Oregon's beet fields. This woman had a heart filled with fresh love for the Lord. As she worked, she would look up into the sky, watching. She thought that any minute she would see Jesus coming down in the clouds.

This same woman still looks up at the blue sky, just as she did then. When she is walking or driving, she glances up at the sky and the clouds. She is still expecting Jesus to return. Like the disciples long ago, we still look up. We hope to meet the Lord in the air at any time.

Dear God, help me to be always ready to meet Jesus when he returns.

PENTECOST

*And everyone present was filled with the Holy Spirit and began speaking
in other languages, as the Holy Spirit gave them this ability.*
ACTS 2:4 NLT

Remember Jesus' promise to the disciples before he went up into
heaven? He promised to send them the Holy Spirit. This happened
on a day called Pentecost.

That day, all the disciples were
gathered in one place. Suddenly
there was a sound like the rush of
a mighty wind. The sound filled
the house where the disciples were
sitting. Then tongues of fire rested
on each of them. This sounds
strange, doesn't it? Something else
came with these tongues of fire.
The disciples had the ability to
speak in different languages!

In the days of the disciples,
Pentecost was a Jewish festival. Thousands of Jews came to Jerusalem
from other countries to celebrate this festival. Many people were in
Jerusalem who spoke different languages. The disciples began to tell
them all about Jesus, speaking in their different languages. The
disciples could do this because of the power of the Holy Spirit.

Peter told them that Jesus had risen from the dead. He said that
they were seeing and hearing the promise of the Father, the Holy
Spirit. It was poured out upon them like water. And about three
thousand people believed in the Lord that day!

Dear God, thank you for sending us your Holy Spirit.

GET UP AND WALK!

The lame man looked at them eagerly, expecting a gift. But Peter said,
"I don't have any money for you. But I'll give you what I have.
In the name of Jesus Christ of Nazareth, get up and walk!"
ACTS 3:5–6 NLT

In America, we have homeless people who live on the streets of our cities. Some of them beg for money from people walking by. In Jerusalem long ago there were also people who had to beg. One of these was a man who couldn't walk. Every day, his friends would carry him to the temple to beg.

One day, Peter and John were going into the temple when the beggar saw them. He held out his hand, hoping for some coins. Instead, both Peter and John looked into his eyes. "Look at us," they said.

The man looked at them, expecting money. But Peter and John had no money. They had something better. They had been filled with the Holy Spirit. In the name of Jesus, they commanded the man to stand up and walk. Suddenly he was so strong that he began leaping. He'd been healed! He ran into the temple, praising God.

My mother is very old and can't walk very well. But each morning she gets out of bed and puts her two feet on the floor, and she thanks God that she can walk at all.

If you're young and healthy, you can run and play. When you do, take a moment to thank God for your strong feet and legs.

Dear God, thank you for giving me strong feet and legs to walk and run and play.

THE APOSTLES' MIRACLES

The apostles performed many miraculous signs
and wonders among the people.
ACTS 5:12 NIV

Jesus healed many people. Later the apostles, filled with the Holy Spirit, did, too. These men gathered every day at a place called Solomon's Porch. There, people learned to believe in the Lord.

Sick people were laid on mats along the streets where the apostles walked. They believed that even a touch from Peter's shadow might heal them. That's how powerful the Holy Spirit is.

All this made the religious leaders (who didn't believe in Jesus) jealous and angry. They arrested the apostles and put them in prison. But this didn't matter. Even though the Lord was no longer on the earth, he was still doing miracles. He sent an angel to open the prison doors. Out came the apostles! At daybreak, they went back to the temple and began teaching again.

Why did the religious leaders throw the apostles in prison? Because the people no longer listened to the religious leaders. Instead, the people believed what the apostles preached.

But wouldn't the religious leaders be happy that people believed in God? No. To them, religion was a business. If people believed the apostles, the religious leaders would lose their jobs.

Dear God, thank you for the apostles who taught us about you.

OBEY GOD FIRST

But an angel of the Lord came at night,
opened the gates of the jail, and brought them out.
Then he told them, "Go to the Temple and give the people this message of life!"
ACTS 5:19–20 NLT

The religious leaders of Israel got together to discuss what to do with the apostles. They sent the temple police to the prison to get them. How surprised they must have been when the police reported to them that the apostles were no longer there! It was strange. The doors of the prison were still firmly locked. The guards were still there, standing at the doors. But there were no apostles inside!

About this time, someone announced that the apostles were in the temple, teaching the people. Ah ha! The religious leaders knew that the apostles were back to preaching.

So the temple police went to the temple to get the apostles. They were brought back to the religious leaders and questioned, "Didn't we give you strict orders not to preach in the name of Jesus?"

But Peter and the other apostles had a good answer. They told the religious leaders that they were going to obey God, not men. This was a very bold answer. Would you give this answer? What if someone wants you to do something that you know is wrong? Remember Peter's answer. You should always obey God first.

Dear God, help me to always obey you before anyone else.

THE FIRST MARTYR

Now Stephen, a man full of God's grace and power,
did great wonders and miraculous signs among the people.

ACTS 6:8 NIV

A believer named Stephen was full of faith and did miracles among the people. But a few men argued with him and even hated him. So they brought him to court and hired people to tell lies about him. As they lied, Stephen's face looked like the face of an angel.

Finally, when Stephen had a chance to speak, he told the history of Israel. The men in the court knew this history already. But when Stephen told it, they realized they didn't believe in God. So they became more furious and ground their teeth with rage.

After his speech, Stephen gazed into heaven and said, "I see the heavens opened. There's Jesus standing at the right hand of God!" Usually the Bible says that Jesus is *sitting* by God. But Stephen saw Jesus standing. This showed that Jesus cared about what was going to happen to Stephen.

Stephen was dragged out of the city. There, people threw stones at him. They hit him with so many stones that Stephen was killed. He was the first Christian martyr. That means he was the first person killed because he lived for Jesus.

Dear God, help me to be like Stephen—to live my life for you, no matter what the cost.

WHEN YOU HURT, JESUS HURTS

As he neared Damascus on his journey,
suddenly a light from heaven flashed around him.
He fell to the ground and heard a voice say to him,
"Saul, Saul, why do you persecute me?"
ACTS 9:3–4 NIV

Saul did his best to destroy the church. One day he was on his way to Damascus to arrest the Christians there. As Saul traveled, a light from heaven flashed around him. Very afraid, he fell to the ground. Then he heard a voice say, "Saul, Saul, why do you persecute me?" To persecute someone is to make them suffer. Saul persecuted Christians because they had a different belief in God than he did.

The voice from heaven asked Saul, "Why do you persecute me?" This voice was speaking from heaven, yet Saul was hurting people on earth.

Saul asked, "Who are you, Lord?"

The voice answered, "I am Jesus." This was a great surprise to Saul. He arrested Jesus' believers on earth. But as he did this, he was persecuting Jesus, who is in heaven. That's because the Lord and his believers are like a human body, and Jesus is the head of that body. When your body gets hurt, your head knows it. You feel hurt. That's how it was with Jesus. When his believers were hurt, Jesus was hurt, too.

Dear God, thank you for knowing when I am hurt. Help me not to hurt others.

"I AM JESUS"

"Who are you, Lord?" Saul asked.
"I am Jesus, whom you are persecuting," he replied.
ACTS 9:5–6 NIV

The man who asked this question was changed forever. If everyone would ask God, "Who are you, Lord?" the world would be a better place.

The man who asked this question was named Saul, later known as Paul. He was born about the same time Jesus was, across the sea from Israel. Paul was sent to Jerusalem to study the religious law of the Jews. As a young man, he was well known by Israel's priests and elders. Paul was a rising star in Jerusalem.

One day, God knocked Paul to the ground and spoke to him. This is when Paul asked, "Who are you, Lord?" God's answer changed him.

The Lord didn't say, "I am the God of your fathers." Paul may have expected him to say, "I am the God of Abraham, Isaac, and Jacob." Rather than this, the Lord said, "I am Jesus of Nazareth."

Paul asked, "Who are you, Lord?" and found that Jesus Christ is God.

"Who are you, Lord?" is a powerful prayer, and God is happy to answer, "I am Jesus Christ."

Dear God, thank you for making it plain who you are—you and Jesus are the same.

CHANGED LIVES

As Saul picked himself up off the ground, he found that he was blind.
So his companions led him by the hand to Damascus.
He remained there blind for three days.

ACTS 9:8–9 NLT

Jesus told Saul to get up from the ground and go to the city. There he would be told what to do. This was quite a change for Saul, a strong and intelligent man. He was used to knowing what to do and doing what he wanted. Now he had to wait to be told what to do next. Not only so, the light had been so bright that Saul had become blind!

The men who journeyed with him had heard the voice, too, but saw no one. They were amazed. They had to take blind Saul by the hand and lead him into Damascus. Although Saul's eyes were open, he could see nothing. In Damascus, he didn't eat or drink anything for three days.

All that happened to Saul tells us what can happen when people come to know Jesus. Big changes come into their lives. A strong man becomes weak. The person who needs no one's help must be led by others. And one's hunger for the things of the world passes away. Jesus becomes the most important thing.

Dear God, thank you for Jesus, who changed my life.

CHOSEN BY GOD

The Lord said, "Go over to Straight Street, to the house of Judas.
When you arrive, ask for Saul of Tarsus. He is praying to me right now.
I have shown him a vision of a man named Ananias coming in
and laying his hands on him so that he can see again."
ACTS 9:11—12 NLT

In the city of Damascus lived a man who followed Jesus. His name was Ananias. The Lord came to Ananias in a vision. A vision is something like a dream except it happens when you're awake. The Lord told Ananias about what had happened to Saul. He told him to go to Straight Street where Saul was staying. Isn't it interesting that Saul was staying on Straight Street? His life had been crooked before this. He was going the wrong way. But the Lord sent Ananias to set Saul on God's straight way.

Ananias didn't want to obey the Lord. He knew what Saul had been doing to Christians like him, how evil he had been, and that Saul had orders to round up all the Christians in Damascus. Ananias was afraid of Saul.

The Lord eased Ananias's fears by telling him of the special plans for Saul. Then Ananias knew that Saul was not a persecutor anymore. Saul had been chosen to bring the gospel to Israel and to the whole world.

Saul's life teaches us many things. The most important is this: When the Lord chooses you, he will make you what he wants you to be. Nothing can stop the Lord from doing this.

Dear God, thank you for choosing me to be your child. Make me who you want me to be.

PAUL'S SUFFERINGS

"I will show him how much he must suffer for my name."
ACTS 9:16 NIV

God chose Saul, who is now known as Paul. Because God chose him, Paul would suffer for the Lord's name, and his suffering started right away.

When Paul first preached in the Jewish synagogues, people knew who he was. "Isn't this the man who persecuted Jesus' followers in Jerusalem?" they asked. "The Christians there were nearly destroyed. We thought that he came here to arrest them. Wasn't he going to take them back to Jerusalem in chains?"

But Paul's preaching became more and more powerful. He told everyone that Jesus was the Messiah. And all the Jews in Damascus couldn't prove him wrong. After a while, the religious leaders decided to kill him. They were watching for Paul at the city gate so they could murder him. But Paul knew about their plot. So during the night, some believers put him in a large basket. They quietly let him down through an opening in the city wall.

At first, Paul had killed the Christians. Then he became a Christian and people wanted to kill him. But no one can kill the truth of the gospel. Paul lived a long life. God protected him so that the gospel of grace could spread around the world.

Dear God, thank you for truth of the gospel. Help me to share it with others, too.

SAUL TO PAUL

So Ananias went and found Saul. He laid his hands on him and said,
"Brother Saul, the Lord Jesus, who appeared to you on the road,
has sent me so that you may get your sight back
and be filled with the Holy Spirit."
ACTS 9:17 NLT

The Lord convinced Ananias to go and see Saul. There, in Judas's house on Straight Street, Ananias found him. He went in the room and touched the blind man.

"Brother Saul," said Ananias, "God sent me so you can see again and be filled with the Spirit." Then a miracle happened. Saul could see again! It was as if scales fell off of his eyes. This was a big experience for Saul, and he never forgot it. Years later he wrote to some Christians and told them of his prayer for them. He prayed that the eyes of their hearts would be opened. He did not want their hearts to be blind like his had been. He wanted the eyes of their hearts to see God's purpose.

Once his sight returned, Saul got baptized and ate some food. Then right away he went out to tell people that Jesus was the Christ, the Son of God. Saul was a changed man! He changed from a persecutor to a preacher. Saul was so different that even his name was changed. He is now known as Paul.

Dear God, please open the eyes of my heart to see you.

THE SHIP OF FAITH

*There they met Timothy, a young disciple whose mother was a Jewish believer,
but whose father was a Greek. Timothy was well thought of by the believers
in Lystra and Iconium, so Paul wanted him to join them on their journey.*

ACTS 16:1–3 NLT

Paul had a young friend named Timothy who sometimes traveled
with him. The New Testament has two books that bear Timothy's
name—1 Timothy and 2 Timothy. They are the letters that Paul
wrote to Timothy.

Paul told Timothy how to help the church in the city where he
lived—to fight to have faith and a good conscience. What is your
conscience? It's a place deep inside you where God lets you know
right from wrong. You know your conscience when you're about to
do something wrong. Then your conscience silently says, "No, don't
do that." Sometimes you don't listen to God's "No" in your conscience. You do the wrong thing anyway. When that happens, you
fall overboard—out of the boat of faith.

If Timothy ignored his conscience, he'd get shipwrecked in the
faith. Paul knew how dangerous it was to be shipwrecked in the sea.
It's even more dangerous if we get shipwrecked in our faith. You
feel far away from the Lord. But Jesus still loves you. Tell him you're
sorry. He'll put you safely back on the ship of faith.

Dear God, help me to always have strong faith and a good conscience.

LYDIA FINDS THE LIGHT

One of them was Lydia from Thyatira, a merchant of expensive purple cloth.
She was a worshiper of God. As she listened to us, the Lord opened her heart,
and she accepted what Paul was saying.

ACTS 16:14 NLT

Paul traveled many places to preach the gospel. One of these places was called Asia. Look for the country called Turkey on a world map. This area was called Asia in Paul's day.

Paul and his friends were traveling through Asia when the Spirit spoke to him. The Spirit said Paul shouldn't speak about Jesus in Asia. So Paul tried to go to Bithynia, but the Spirit wouldn't allow this. Paul didn't know where to go. Then he had a vision in the night. In his vision was a man from Macedonia begging him to come there. So Paul sailed to Philippi, a large city in Macedonia. He stayed there several days.

That weekend, Paul and his friends went outside the city to a river, looking for a place to pray. Women were gathering there. Lydia was one of these women. She was a businesswoman from the town of Thyatira who sold purple cloth. Maybe she had come to the river to sell some cloth. No one knows why Lydia was at the river that day.

We do know that the Bible says Lydia was a worshiper of God. Lydia had a heart for God. We also know that the name *Lydia* is Greek meaning "light." So this story is about a woman who was searching for the true light of God.

Dear God, help me to be like Lydia, searching for your light.

HOSPITALITY

When she and the members of her household were baptized,
she invited us to her home. "If you consider me a believer in the Lord,"
she said, "come and stay at my house."

ACTS 16:15 NIV

Lydia may have heard Paul and his friends praying. God opened her heart and she listened eagerly to what Paul had to say. Then she was baptized. They didn't have to go far for this. They were already beside a river!

Lydia had been trying to make money selling her purple cloth. But now she wanted to spend her money for the gospel of grace. She urged Paul and all of his friends to come to her home. She wanted to give them hospitality while they were in Macedonia.

Later Paul wrote about hospitality: "When God's children are in need, be the one to help them out. And get into the habit of inviting guests home for dinner or, if they need lodging, for the night."

Lydia is a good example of someone who gives hospitality. Giving hospitality is a good deed that helps those who are traveling. Do you have friends come to your house for dinner? Do your relatives come and spend the night at your house sometimes? When this happens, you are giving hospitality just as Paul asked you to do.

Dear God, help me to give hospitality to others.

AFRAID? TRY SINGING

Around midnight, Paul and Silas were praying and singing hymns to God,
and the other prisoners were listening.
ACTS 16:25 NLT

It was not very comfortable for Paul and Silas in the prison in Philippi. Awake at midnight, they sang to God.

Sometimes you might feel that you are in an invisible prison of

feelings. You may feel sad, afraid, or alone. You may feel like there is no way out of these feelings. But like Paul and Silas, you can sing. Even a simple song like "This Little Light of Mine" can unlock the door of sadness or fear.

Last summer I visited Yosemite National Park. Late in the afternoon, I stopped to see some giant sequoia trees. In the parking lot, there were signs that warned about mountain lions. But even though I was alone, I hiked up a trail to see a huge tree. Unfortunately, the hike took longer than I expected, and darkness was falling as I came back down the trail.

Hurrying along, I thought I saw something jump from a nearby stump. I heard a crashing noise. Was it a mountain lion? My heart pounded with fear as I nearly ran down the trail. Loudly, I sang, "Surely goodness and mercy will follow me, all the days of my life. . . ." I reached the parking lot with thanks to God. My singing gave me courage to escape my fear of an unseen mountain lion.

Dear God, help me to sing to you when I am afraid.

FAMiLY SALVATiON

The jailer called for lights, rushed in and fell trembling before Paul and Silas.
He then brought them out and asked, "Sirs, what must I do to be saved?"
They replied, "Believe in the Lord Jesus, and you will be saved—
you and your household." Then they spoke the word of the Lord
to him and to all the others in his house.

ACTS 16:29–32 NIV

These verses show that God cares about you *and* your family. The jailer in Philippi awoke to find all the prison doors open. He thought all his prisoners had escaped. So he was about to kill himself. But Paul called to him, "All the prisoners are still here." What a miracle that was!

Then the jailer asked Paul and Silas, "What must I do to be saved?"

They told him to believe in Jesus. If he did this, he *and his household* would be saved.

Have you ever set up dominoes in a wavy line and then pushed the first one over? It knocks the next domino over. That one knocks over the next, until the entire line is knocked over. That's what household salvation in this story is like. When someone believes in Jesus, they tell someone else in their family about him. Then that person believes and tells another family member. This is how an entire household comes to know Jesus. This happened in my family. I believed in Jesus. Then my mother and father, my sister, and my other sister believed. Next, my grandparents and my aunt came to him. And it's not over yet—I still have cousins who are going to believe!

Dear God, thank you for loving my family. Help them all to know you.

LORD AND KING

*"Paul and Silas have turned the rest of the world upside down,
and now they are here disturbing our city," they shouted.
"And Jason has let them into his home.
They are all guilty of treason against Caesar,
for they profess allegiance to another king, Jesus."*

ACTS 17:6–7 NLT

Paul and his friends were called "those that turned the world upside down." The preaching of the good news caused uproar wherever Paul went. Town by town, the world was being changed—turned upside down. Paul proclaimed Jesus as the Messiah and King. Some believed and some did not. Even though some did not believe, that did not change the fact that Jesus is the King.

As I write this, it is the year 2004. You may be reading this book in 2005. These years are sometimes called 2004 AD or 2005 AD The letters AD are short for the Latin words *anno domini*. This means, "The year of our Lord."

Nearly two thousand years have passed since Paul began preaching the good news about Jesus. Some people have believed the gospel and some have not yet believed. But everyone in the world is living in the year of our Lord. Since he is the owner of this year, he is everyone's King. He is the King of all years and of all ages. Here is a way you can praise him: "Glory and honor to God forever and ever. He is the eternal King, the unseen one who never dies; he alone is God."

NOBLE BELIEVERS

Now the Bereans were of more noble character than the Thessalonians,
for they received the message with great eagerness and examined
the Scriptures every day to see if what Paul said was true.
ACTS 17:11 NIV

Do you know anyone who reads the Bible every day? Maybe your mother or father read and study it. I hope so. Why do they read that same book day after day? It is because the Bible is food for their souls.

You eat food every day to be healthy, right? Healthy Christians eat the living Word of God every day. This makes them spiritually healthy.

As Christians, we should eat the living Word of God. This means reading and studying the Bible, praying, and talking with others about the Bible. In this way, we eat the Word of God.

Israel's prophet, Jeremiah, spoke about eating God's Word: "When your words came, I ate them; they were my joy and my heart's delight, for I bear your name, O LORD God Almighty."

I think that the people in Berea had a taste for God's Word, the Bible. Paul came to them with the good news about Jesus Christ. This was something they had never heard before. But they didn't send him away. They read, studied, and prayed about his message as they searched the scriptures. In this way, they were nobler than their neighbors, the Thessalonians.

I hope you grow up to be a noble Christian.

Dear God, help me to be noble by studying your Word.

KNOWING THE UNKNOWN GOD

So Paul. . .addressed them as follows: "Men of Athens,
I notice that you are very religious, for as I was walking along I saw your many altars.
And one of them had this inscription on it—'To an Unknown God.'
You have been worshiping him without knowing who he is,
and now I wish to tell you about him."

ACTS 17:22–23 NLT

Paul walked around Athens and saw how the people worshiped. They worshiped idols—false gods. The people of Athens even had an altar to an unknown god! There they worshiped something, but

they didn't know what it was. So Paul told them about the God they didn't know. He said this God is the Creator who made the world and everything in it. Paul told them that God had decided when each of them would be born. He told them why they were born—to seek God and find him. He told them that God is not far from any of us because in him we live, move, and exist.

Most people don't realize they're living and moving in God. They don't know they were born to seek God and find God. But God is not far from them, and he wants to be found by them. God created a craving for himself in every human being. As we move through this life, his mercy makes us aware of this craving. So we seek after God and find him. This is what God wants for everyone.

Dear God, help me to seek you and find you.

REACH OUT TO GOD

"From one man he made every nation of men,
that they should inhabit the whole earth; and he determined
the times set for them and the exact places where they should live.
God did this so that men would seek him and perhaps reach out for him
and find him, though he is not far from each one of us."
ACTS 17:26–27 NIV

There are many nations on this earth. Each has millions of people and all are different. However, each person is the same as everyone else in one way: We all have blood, which gives us life. This blood is the same as the blood of the first man, Adam.

The first book of the Bible, Genesis, tells about Adam. God created him from the dust of the ground and breathed into him. So Adam became a living soul. Then Adam lived in the Garden of Eden, keeping it safe and beautiful. Mankind doesn't live in a garden anymore. Still, we all must work to live and keep the earth safe.

But this is not the reason we are here. God's purpose for our lives is much more than this. In the garden, Adam and Eve spoke with God and heard his voice. God walked with them in the cool of the day. In other words, they enjoyed being with God, walking and talking with him each day.

We are here to search for God, reach out for him, and find him. And God is never far from any one of us.

Dear God, thank you for always being close to me.

DARKNESS TO LIGHT

A number who had practiced sorcery brought their scrolls together
and burned them publicly. When they calculated the value of the scrolls,
the total came to fifty thousand drachmas.
In this way the word of the Lord spread widely and grew in power.
ACTS 19:19–20 NIV

Paul came to the city of Ephesus and told them about Jesus. The people who became believers there turned from their evil ways. They no longer wanted to practice magic. They collected all their books about magic and burned them. This was wise of them. These books would have stopped them from growing in the Lord.

Paul wrote a letter to the believers in Ephesus. In it, he told them, "Once you were darkness." This means that they weren't only in the darkness, they were darkness itself! All the things they learned from their curious books made them dark. No wonder they burned those books!

When the Ephesians believed in Jesus, they became light in the Lord. So Paul encouraged them to live like children of light. "This light grows into good and right and true things," he wrote. "So find out what is pleasing to the Lord. Have nothing to do with the worthless deeds of evil and darkness. It is shameful even to talk about such things. Be careful how you live. Be wise, not foolish. Do good whenever you can, because these are evil days."

A MAN NAMED EUTYCHUS

Seated in a window was a young man named Eutychus,
who was sinking into a deep sleep as Paul talked on and on.
When he was sound asleep, he fell to the ground from the third story
and was picked up dead.

ACTS 20:9 NIV

One Sunday, the church in Troas gathered to eat a meal. Paul was there with them, and he preached until midnight.

Many flickering lamps were lighting the third-floor room. A young man named Eutychus was sleepily sitting on the windowsill. Finally, in a deep sleep, he fell to his death on the street below.

Paul ran downstairs to the street and bent over the young man. Taking him in his arms, he said, "Don't worry, he's alive!"

Then they all went back upstairs and ate together. Paul continued talking to them until dawn, and then he left. Meanwhile, the young man was taken home. He wasn't even hurt, and everyone was very thankful.

This story tells us about God's gift of salvation. Many people are like Eutychus. He was young and not interested in Paul's preaching. So on the edge of the gathering, he fell asleep. Then he fell to his death.

Many people are not only asleep like Eutychus, they're also dead in spirit. But this doesn't matter to God. He makes us alive through Christ just like Paul brought Eutychus to life. This is a picture of God's grace.

Dear God, thank you for your grace, which brings us from death to life.

PAUL'S TRIAL

*The weather was becoming dangerous for long voyages by then
because it was so late in the fall, and Paul spoke to the ship's officers about it.
"Sirs," he said, "I believe there is trouble ahead if we go on—shipwreck,
loss of cargo, injuries, and danger to our lives." But the officer in charge of the
prisoners listened more to the ship's captain and the owner than to Paul.*

ACTS 27:9–11 NLT

The apostle Paul was arrested for telling people about Jesus. He had to go to Rome, Italy, to stand trial. Paul and some other prisoners were taken to a ship and they sailed

away. On the sea, the ship ran into headwinds. This made it hard for the ship to stay on course. After days of rough sailing and great difficulty, they finally arrived at Fair Havens. The weather was dangerous for long trips because it was so late in the fall.

So Paul spoke to the ship's officers. "Sirs," he said, "I think there is trouble ahead if we go on. There will be a shipwreck, loss of cargo, injuries, and danger to our lives." But the officer in charge of the prisoners didn't listen to Paul.

Fair Havens was a poor place to spend the winter. A light wind began blowing from the south, so the ship tried to get to Phoenix, farther up the coast. But the weather changed and a powerful wind blew the ship out to sea. The sailors lost control of the ship. It was driven by the wind.

The terrible storm raged for many days. It blotted out the sun and the stars. At last, all hope was gone.

Dear God, help me to be brave when I am afraid of bad storms.

GOD'S PROTECTION

Paul called the crew together and said,
"Men, you should have listened to me in the first place and not left Fair Havens.
You would have avoided all this injury and loss.
But take courage! None of you will lose your lives,
even though the ship will go down."

ACTS 27:21–22 NLT

The ship was in danger of sinking in the storm. No one had eaten for a long time. Paul called the crew together and said, "None of you will die, even though the ship will sink. Last night an angel of my God stood beside me. He said, 'Don't be afraid. God in his goodness has given safety to everyone sailing with you.'

"So be brave!" Paul said, "I believe God. It will be just as he said. But we will be shipwrecked on an island."

It was midnight on the fourteenth night of the storm. The sailors knew land was near. They found the water was very shallow, and they were afraid the ship would hit the rocks along the shore. So they threw out four anchors and prayed for daylight. Then the sailors were so afraid that they tried to leave the ship. They lowered the lifeboat. But Paul said to the captain, "You will all die unless the sailors stay on the ship." So they let the lifeboat fall off.

The darkness passed and early morning light appeared. Paul begged everyone to eat. "You haven't eaten for two weeks," he said. "Please eat. Not a hair of your heads will be lost."

Dear God, thank you for protecting us from bad storms.

GOD CAN SAVE

But the ship hit a shoal and ran aground. . . .
The soldiers wanted to kill the prisoners to make sure they didn't swim ashore
and escape. But the commanding officer wanted to spare Paul,
so he didn't let them carry out their plan. . . .
So everyone escaped safely ashore!
ACTS 27:41–44 NLT

There were 276 people who ate on board the ship that day. Then the crew made the ship lighter. They threw the cargo of wheat overboard.

Morning dawned, and they didn't know where they were. But they saw a bay with a beach. *Can we get between the rocks and get the ship safely to shore?* they wondered.

So they cut off the anchors and left them in the sea. Then they lowered the rudders, raised the sail, and headed toward shore. But the ship ran aground. The bow of the ship stuck fast. The stern was smashed by the waves and began to break apart.

The soldiers wanted to kill Paul and the other prisoners so they couldn't escape. But the captain wanted Paul to live. He didn't let the soldiers carry out their plan. Then he ordered all who could swim to jump overboard and swim for land. The others floated on planks from the broken ship. Everyone escaped safely ashore!

Everyone on board that ship lived because of Paul. He believed that God would save them.

Dear God, thank you for saving Paul and all the men on the ship.

WORDS OF LiFE

Yet faith comes from listening to this message of good news—
the Good News about Christ.
ROMANS 10:17 NLT

"Your word is a lamp for my feet and a light for my path," said a poet in the Bible. This means that that God's Word is a light to guide you into faith in God. The same poet said, "As your words are taught, they give light; even the simple can understand them." The Bible will take you out of darkness and into light. It tells us all about God, who is light.

The stories in the four gospels are fun to read. But much of the Bible is deep and mysterious. The book of Romans is like this. When you read it, there may be things you don't understand, but don't worry about that.

The Bible contains the words of life. Jesus said, "The words I speak to you are spirit and life." Not only so, the Bible says God's Word does not return to him empty. It does what he wants it to do. I think this means that whatever you read in the Bible will give you life. If you do not understand it now, that is okay. As you grow older, God will give you understanding.

Dear God, help me to understand your Word.

LIKE A SEED

I passed on to you what was most important
and what had also been passed on to me—that Christ died for our sins,
just as the Scriptures said. He was buried,
and he was raised from the dead on the third day.

1 CORINTHIANS 15:3–4 NLT

How do we know that Christ's death on the cross did away with sin? Because Jesus didn't stay dead! God raised him from the dead. It's an amazing thing, and it's hard even for adults to understand. How could a dead man come back to life?

God has given us an example of resurrection that we can see in nature. A seed is a tiny thing. It's not alive. But when you plant that seed in your garden and give it water and sunshine, soon a plant grows! Jesus even compared himself to a type of seed—a grain of wheat. Before his resurrection, he told his disciples, "Unless a grain of wheat falls into the earth and dies, it remains a single grain. But if it dies, it bears much fruit."

When Jesus lived in Israel, he was like a single grain of wheat. Then he died and was resurrected from the dead. By his death, your sin was taken away. You and all of Jesus' believers are like many grains of wheat. Because he was resurrected, you, too, will be resurrected.

Dear God, thank you for bringing Jesus back to life. Thank you that I will come back to life, too.

JARS OF CLAY

But we have this treasure in jars of clay to show that
this all-surpassing power is from God and not from us.
2 CORINTHIANS 4:7 NIV

The New Testament book of 2 Corinthians explains Paul's life. It shows that whatever he accomplished was not his own work. It was all thanks to God. This is why he didn't preach himself. He proclaimed Jesus Christ as Lord.

Jesus called Paul a "chosen vessel." In 2 Corinthians Paul talks about this. A vessel is a bowl, a jar, or a bottle. Paul said that he was like a clay jar. Such a jar had little value unless it was filled—just like a carton of orange juice. You keep the carton because it has juice in it. When the juice is gone, you throw away the carton. That is how Paul saw himself. He was just a vessel, but he was filled with a treasure. The treasure is Christ. So the amazing power in Paul's life was not his own. It was from God who was in him like sweet juice in a carton.

Would you like Christ to be in you? You can pray one of Paul's own prayers: "I pray that Christ be at home in my heart as I trust in him. May the roots of my life grow deep into the soil of God's great love."

Dear God, please let Christ be at home in my heart. Make me a vessel filled with you.

CROWNS

You know how full of love and kindness our Lord Jesus Christ was.
Though he was very rich, yet for your sakes he became poor,
so that by his poverty he could make you rich.

2 CORINTHIANS 8:9 NLT

Every king has a crown. Most crowns are made of gold and precious jewels, but Jesus Christ's crown was made of thorns. We try to rid our world of thorns. We chop, burn, gather, and dump them. But weeds, brambles, and choking vines return to our land year after year. Tumbleweeds line our fences no matter how hard we try to destroy them.

Rock miners didn't have to dig to find the material for Christ's crown. Jewelers didn't have to cut and polish gems to decorate his head. The Bible says, "They made a crown of long, sharp thorns and put it on his head, and they placed a stick in his right hand as a scepter. Then they knelt before him in mockery, yelling, 'Hail! King of the Jews!'"

Long before this, God told Adam and Eve, "I have cursed the ground. It will grow thorns for you." Today we still have thorns growing all around. We can't get rid of them. But our curse became Christ's crown, and he saved us from our sins.

Dear God, thank you for bearing our crown of thorns by sending Jesus to save us.

THE SWORD OF THE SPIRIT

Take the helmet of salvation and the sword of the Spirit,
which is the word of God.

EPHESIANS 6:17 NIV

I've been reading the Bible for over thirty years. And I'm happy and excited these days because I've recently understood it better. I've seen more of who God is and what he has done in his grace.

I like to read, and I read many things. But the Bible is the only book I've read every day for over half my life. I never grow tired of it. It is an endless gift that I unwrap a little more every day. What a beautiful gift from God!

I trust in God that I'll never grow bored with the Bible. I have two friends who are eighty-six years old. They have been reading the Bible since they were children. Dorothy has gone blind, so her husband Chuck reads to her every day. My wife and I visit them on Sundays, and together we study the Bible. This is the best time we have all week.

There is no other book on the earth like the Bible. You can read it every day for a hundred years. Chuck and Dorothy have nearly done this. They will tell you that it is always fresh, full of light, and even delicious! They happily say to God, "To me, your word is the joy and rejoicing of my heart."

Dear God, help me always to find joy in your Word.

DON'T WORRY—PRAY

Don't worry about anything; instead, pray about everything.
Tell God what you need, and thank him for all he has done.
If you do this, you will experience God's peace.

PHILIPPIANS 4:6–7 NLT

Think of the billions of people who've lived since these words were written. Each one had friends, family, joys, and sadness. Yet the Bible presents everyone with the same advice: Don't worry about anything. Instead, give thanks and pray.

This is amazing! And even better, an answer to all such prayer is guaranteed. This answer may not be what you expect, though. Instead of a direct reply, God gives the praying person peace through Christ. This echoes the words of Jesus: "I'm leaving peace with you. I give my peace to you. Don't let your heart be troubled, or let it be afraid."

No one can understand the peace of God, but you can experience it. Peace is as real as God. God is known as the God of peace who gives you peace at all times in all ways. We Christians believe in the God of peace, who brought our Lord Jesus back from the dead. To experience the God of peace we have to do only one thing, and that is pray.

The Bible says you shouldn't worry about anything. Instead, pray about everything. Tell God what you need, and give thanks. If you do this, you'll experience God's peace.

Dear God, help me to pray to you for everything—and give me your peace.

THE GIFT OF PEACE

And let the peace that comes from Christ rule in your hearts.
For as members of one body you are all called to live in peace.
And always be thankful.
COLOSSIANS 3:15 NLT

Jesus said, "I am leaving you with a gift—peace of mind and heart. And the peace I give isn't like the peace the world gives. So don't be troubled or afraid."

Ever since the times of Jesus, peace has been compared with a dove. This bird is also a symbol of the Holy Spirit. When the Spirit came down upon Jesus, it looked like a dove. The Holy Spirit gives us God's peace.

Because Christians have God's Spirit, we don't worry about anything. Instead, we pray about everything. In prayer, we tell God what we need, and we thank him for all things. This brings us God's peace. This peace is impossible to explain. It is far more wonderful than your mind can understand. Let this peace guard your heart and mind as you live in Christ.

Doves are very shy. It is easy to scare them away. This is true with peace, too. It can come and go like a bird. One day, Jesus will bring his peace to the earth to stay forever. He will bring the kingdom of peace.

Dear God, I thank you that one day you'll bring peace to the earth.

THE REWARD

And now the prize awaits me—the crown of righteousness that the Lord,
the righteous Judge, will give me on that great day of his return.
And the prize is not just for me but for all who eagerly
look forward to his glorious return.

2 TIMOTHY 4:8 NLT

Jesus once said, "A wheat seed must fall into the ground and die. If it doesn't, it will always be a single seed. But if it dies, it produces many seeds." When you believe in Jesus, you become like one of

these wheat seeds. This is a picture of what Jesus has done by dying and coming back from death.

All of the people who have ever believed in Jesus are like wheat seeds. Death will not be able to hold them, either. They will come to life just as a seed does when it is planted.

Jesus Christ was righteous. When you believe, you are made righteous, too. Someday, Jesus will come back and you will welcome him. Then God will not judge you. Instead, you will be blessed. This blessing is like a crown. The apostle Paul looked forward to that day. So he said, "From now on God has set aside the crown of righteousness for me. The Lord, who is the righteous judge, will give it to me on that day. He will not only give it to me but also to all who have longed for him to return."

Dear God, thank you for blessing me and making me righteous through Jesus.

THE LIVING LORD

His head and his hair were white like wool,
as white as snow. And his eyes were bright like flames of fire.
REVELATION 1:14 NLT

No one today really knows what Jesus looked like. But one old man described him in the Bible. John, who lived on a little island called Patmos about sixty-five years after Jesus died, had a vision of the Lord. He saw the resurrected Jesus.

John was praying on a Sunday when he heard a voice behind him—it turned out to be Jesus Christ. John wrote that Jesus was wearing a long robe with a gold sash across his chest. His hair was woolly, as white as snow. His eyes flashed like fire. His feet were like pure, shining bronze. His voice thundered like ocean waves that break on the shore. Seven stars were in his right hand, and a sharp sword came out of his mouth. His face was as bright as the sun on a perfectly clear day.

When John saw Jesus, he fainted. But Jesus said, "Don't be afraid! I am the first, the last, and the living one. I was dead, and look, I'm alive forever and ever!"

Think of that! Jesus is alive right now. He is holding and loving us like those seven bright stars in his hand.

Dear God, thank you for being our wonderful and living Lord!

NEW JERUSALEM

Then I saw a new heaven and a new earth. . . . And I saw the holy city,
the new Jerusalem, coming down from God out of heaven.
REVELATION 21:1–2 NLT

Do you know how the Bible ends? In the end, heaven comes to earth. John saw this in his vision. It is a holy city named the New Jerusalem. It will come down out of heaven from God. This city is like a beautiful bride who is ready to marry her husband.

John heard a voice coming from God's throne. "Look," the voice said. "The home of God is now among people! He will live with them. They will be his people. God will be with them. All their tears will be wiped away. There will be no more death, sorrow, crying, or pain. The old world is gone forever."

Then the one sitting on the throne said, "Look, I am making everything new!"

This wonderful city of God is the hope of every Christian. We will all be there living with God on the new earth.

This is God's promise: "It is finished! I'm the Alpha and the Omega—the beginning and the end. I will freely give the thirsty people water from the spring of the water of life. I'll be their God and they'll be my children."

Dear God, thank you for your glory that lasts forever and ever!

A BEAUTIFUL FOREVER

"These words are trustworthy and true: 'The Lord God,
who tells his prophets what the future holds,
has sent his angel to tell you what will happen soon.'"

REVELATION 22:6 NLT

The last two chapters of the Bible are a picture. They describe the beauty and joy of eternity with God. An angel explained to John what this is like.

"The angel showed me a pure river full of the water of life," wrote John. "It flows clear as crystal from the throne of God and of the Lamb. The river streams down the center of the street. The tree of life grows on each side of the river. It bears twelve kinds of fruit, one during each month of the year. The tree of life's leaves are used as medicine to heal the nations."

"Nothing there is accursed because the throne of God and of the Lamb is there. God's servants worship him and see his face. Not only so, God's name is written on their foreheads. There is no night in the New Jerusalem, so there is no need for lamps or sunshine. The Lord God shines on the people and they reign forever and ever."

These words of the Bible paint a real and beautiful picture of what is waiting for us. As the angel told John, "These words are trustworthy and true."

Dear God, thank you that everything you say is trustworthy and true.

ABOUT THE AUTHOR

DANIEL PARTNER, a veteran Christian author and editor, lives in Coos Bay, Oregon. His books include *I Give Myself to Prayer, All Things Are Possible, Peace Like a River, Women of Sacred Song* (written with his wife, Margaret), and *The One-Year Book of Poetry* (coedited with Philip Comfort). All are available at Christian bookstores nationwide.

Besides his publishing work, Daniel is active in preserving and performing mid-nineteenth-century American popular music. Contact him by e-mail at author@danpartner.com.